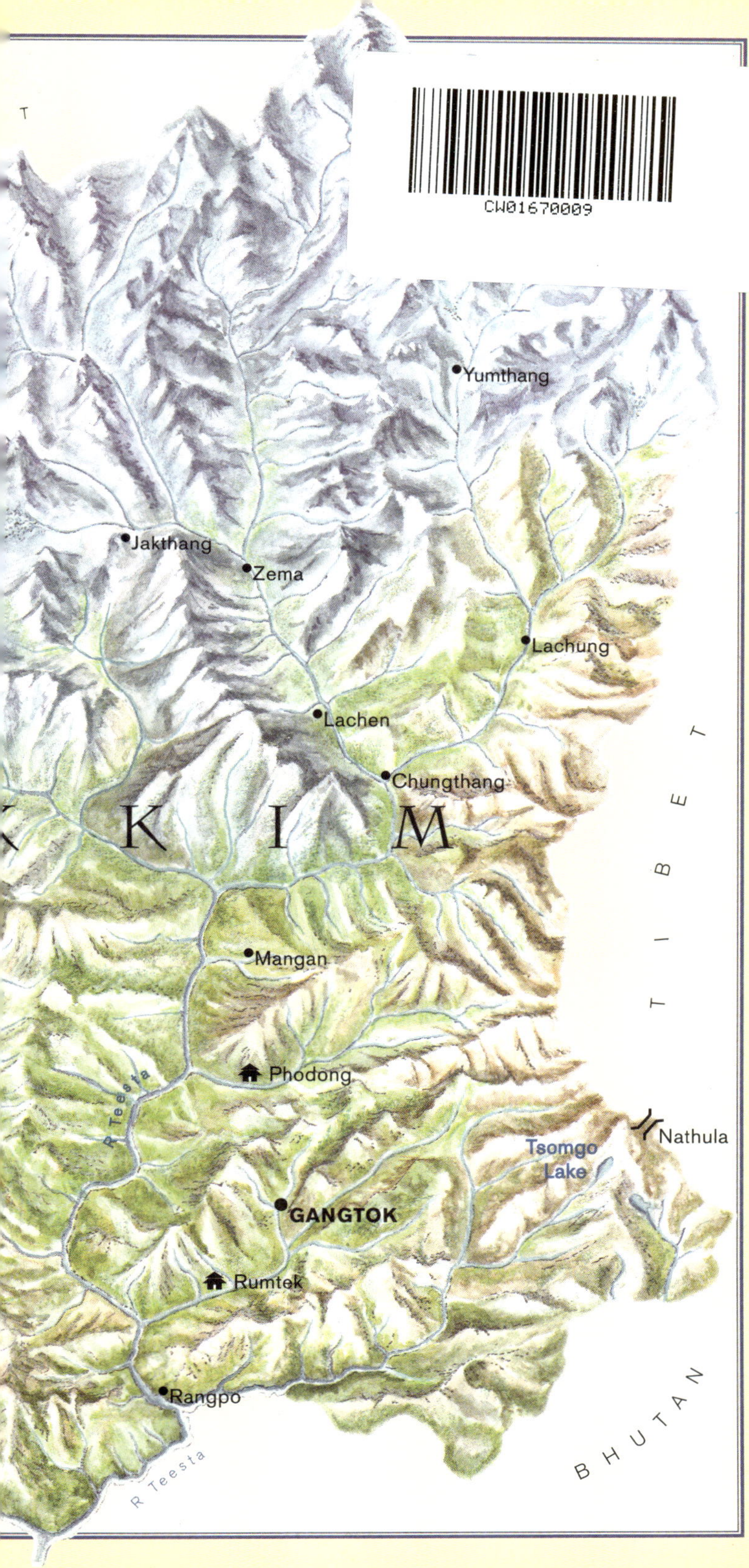

T
Yumthang
Jakthang
Zema
Lachung
Lachen
Chungthang
K I M
T I B E T
Mangan
Phodong
R Teesta
Nathula
Tsomgo Lake
GANGTOK
Rumtek
Rangpo
R Teesta
BHUTAN

SIKKIM
LAND OF MYSTIQUE

EICHER GOODEARTH LIMITED, New Delhi
Supported by
Sikkim Tourism
&
Department of Tourism, Government of India

A GOOD EARTH PUBLICATION

ISBN 81-87780-13-4

Editor and Publisher: Swati Mitra
Senior Editor: Sona Thakur
Design: Ayesha Sarkar, Sudhir John Horo & Alpana Khare

Photographs:
Ashok Dilwali pp. 4, 6, 8, 16-17, 18Below Left, 26-27, 36, 43, 62, 80, 81, 84, 103Below, 106, 113Above, 114-15, 116, 119, 122, 126, 130, 138, 152, 161A
Arindam Sen Gupta pp. 14, 19Middle, 40A, 44, 55, 58, 60A, 74A, 78, 82, 88, 98, 101A, 112B, 113B, 118, 121
Darshan Singh pp. 10, 12, 18Below Right, 19B, 29, 32, 52, 57, 61, 64, 74B, 76, 88, 89, 90A, 92, 94, 97, 104A, 120A, 125, 142
Guru Ladakhi pp. 30, 49, 67; Swati Mitra pp. 34, 74A, 120B, 128, 135, 155B, 156A;
Kuldeep Mukhia pp. 70-71; Ayesha Sarkar pp. 48A, 87A;
AGP Photobank pp. 11, 38, 40B, 50, 68, 86, 91
Illustrations: Neelkant Chaudhary pp. 20-25
Special thanks to
Karma Gyatso, IAS, & P K Dong of Sikkim Tourism

The Publishers would be happy to receive suggestions and corrections for inclusion in the next edition. Please write to:
Head of Publishing, Eicher Goodearth Ltd,
Eicher House, 12 Commercial Complex,
Greater Kailash II (Masjid Moth),
New Delhi 110 048.

This publication has been supported by
Sikkim Tourism & Department of Tourism, Government of India

Printed by Ajanta Offset & Packaging Ltd, New Delhi
on behalf of Eicher Goodearth Ltd

Price: Rs 220

CONTENTS

LOCATING SIKKIM

The Khang-chen-dzonga presides over Sikkim as its guardian deity. Its five peaks stand over the state like a palm held up in perpetual blessing. For the people of Sikkim, then, Khang-chen-dzonga is more than just the third highest peak in the world; it is believed to be the abode of the state's patron deity. According to popular belief, the red-robed god guards Sikkim and its people from all harm.

A full view of the Khang-chen-dzonga range
Previous Page: The Khang-chen-dzonga as seen from Dzongri in West Sikkim

Khang-chen-dzonga, literally FiveTreasures of the Eternal Snow, is believed to be the storehouse of all that is precious. In the words of Lama Lhatsun Chempo, the 17th century holy man who anointed the first Chogyal of Sikkim: 'The peak most conspicuously gilded by the rising sun is the treasury of gold; the peak that remains in cold grey shade is the storehouse for silver; and the other peaks are vaults for gems, grains and the holy books'.

Topography

The snow-sheathed Khang-chen-dzonga dominates both the thoughtscape and the landscape of Sikkim. Forming the northwest border with Nepal, the mountain and its attendant range keep the rain-laden clouds of the southwest monsoon from wandering beyond Sikkim.

Sikkim is like a stupendous stairway leading from the western border of the Tibetan plateau down to the plains of West Bengal, with a fall of about 5,215 metres in 240 kms. The surface of this rough incline is scoured with deep gorges, down which rush glacial waters, swollen by the excessive rainfall of this, the wettest section of the Himalayas.

The Lachung valley in North Sikkim wreathed in mist

By virtue of its location close to the equator and to the Bay of Bengal, Sikkim enjoys an uncannily tropical climate in the lower reaches.

The state lies like an amphitheatre, open towards the south, between the Singalila and Chola ranges to the west and east respectively. The two ranges also form the watersheds of the Rangeet and the Teesta rivers, while subsidiary spurs radiate from these ranges, serving as separate watersheds for the Lachung, Lachen, Zemu, Tholung, Rongli and Rongpo rivers. The rivers together make a fan-like formation, converging at the bottom into the Teesta.

The Teesta

The Teesta is born near the pristine waters of the Tso Lhamu Lake on a plateau in the farthest north of Sikkim, some 5,300 metres above sea level. The glacial waters then slice southwards to meet the Zemu Chu just above Lachen village.

Cascading down through deep gorges, it meets the Lachung Chu at Chungthang. The river has come barely 80 kms from its source but has already dropped some 4,000 metres in a series of stunning waterfalls. Its waters doubled, the Teesta thunders down to collect the Tolung Chu at Mangan, before losing much of its force at Singtam where it slows and broadens and becomes navigable for the first time. The stretch of the river between Singtam and Rangpo is a popular rafting tract.

At Rangpo, the river turns west forming the border between the states of Sikkim and West Bengal. At Melli, the Teesta merges its sediment-heavy waters with the lighter stream of the Rangeet that was born in the Rathong glacier in West Sikkim. The swollen waters then flow slowly to join with the Brahmaputra in Bangladesh.

From the valley floor, watered by the fast-flowing Teesta, terraced rice fields rise in amazing shades of green, giving Sikkim its other name of *Beyul Demozong* or Hidden Valley of Rice. The green paddy terraces give way to rugged mountains studded with gem-like lakes and sparkling waterfalls.

The icy source of the Teesta, Sikkim's mightiest river
Below: The tropical lushness of the meandering Teesta

Gurudongmar Lake in North Sikkim is held in deep reverence. Locals leave little pyramids of stones here as marks of their devotion.

Altitudes rise towards the north, where, amid steep ridges, are born many rivers that run through incredibly deep gorges seaming the face of the land.

In fact, Sikkim's tortuous rivers carry tropical vegetation far into the mountains of the interior until you have the strange situation of tropical undergrowth flourishing in the very shadow of snow-capped peaks.

Sikkim is also known for the steepest rise in altitude over the shortest distance. The rise in height from mean sea level to the top of Khang-chen-dzonga at 8,586 metres is achieved in 80 kms as the crow flies. Altitudes in the state vary from 253 metres to 8,595 metres, giving Sikkim its unique climate. Within its 7,300 sq kms lies the entire climatic range: from tropical to temperate to alpine.

Caves of Sikkim

The mountains of Sikkim are studded with caves and most of them are held sacred by the locals. Lamas retreat into them to meditate and pilgrims enter their dark depths to light butter lamps of devotion. Of the four caves considered the most sacred, the holiest is *Lharinyingphu* or the Old Cave of God's Hill which can be accessed only by a three-day trek from Tashiding. Then there is *Dechenphu* or Cave of Happiness and *Sharchok Pephu* or Secret Cave close to Ravangla and *Khandrosamphu* or the Cave of Fairies on the road to Pemayangtse.

Districts

Sikkim is divided into four districts. They are North Sikkim with its headquarter at Mangan, South Sikkim head-quartered at Namchi Bazaar, West Sikkim with its base at Gyaltshing and East Sikkim with its head-quarters at Gangtok, which is also the state capital.

Strings of prayer flags fluttering in the breeze are an abiding part of Sikkim's landscape

Ecosystem

The awesome topographical variety makes Sikkim a virtual laboratory for the study of ecosystems. The British naturalist Dr Joseph Dalton Hooker spent several years in Sikkim in the 19th century and his material, compiled in *Himalayan Journal*, proved invaluable for Charles Darwin in his study of the origin of species.

Botanically, Sikkim has an amazing diversity to offer. To begin with, 36 per cent of the state is forested, which makes for a wonderful contrast with the other fast-denuding hill states of India. The lowlands of the south have figs, laurel, sal and bamboo trees. The temperate forests of oak, chestnut, maple, birch, silver fir, bamboo, teak and sal dominate the middle heights, while the alpine forests of juniper, cypress and rhododendron green the area just below the snowline.

Orchid

An awesome 600 species of this most exotic of flowers can be found in Sikkim. *Dendrobium, Cattaleya, Cymbidium, Vanda* – all the famous families can be found in their natural habitat in a rainbow range of colours. The most common of the lot, the *Dendrobium Nobile* has been adopted by the state as its official flower.

Polybag-free State

Sikkim is blazing a trail in environment consciousness. The government has declared the state a polybag-free state and you will find none of the offending non-biodegradable packaging in the state.

Fauna

The animal life of Sikkim is equally varied. A number of exotic animals like the shapi (the Himalayan tahr), red panda, musk deer, snow leopard, blue sheep, and the massive Himalayan bear roam its slopes. There have also been reports of Yeti sightings. This mythical creature is called *Migyud* by the Sikkimese. The state also has over 400 types of butterflies and 550 species of birds.

From Top: A flowering magnolia tree, snow leopard, and the Himalayan bear
Opposite Page: Some of the innumerable orchids found on Sikkim's slopes

Flora

But Sikkim's actual wealth is in its flowers. When Dr Hooker tabulated them some 150 years ago, there were 2,920 species. Primulas, poppies and gentians all run a riot of colour in spring but pride of place is reserved for the orchids and rhododendrons. Of the 5,000 species of orchids known in the world, 600 can be found in the lower reaches of Sikkim alone. As for rhododendrons, you can find more than 300 species here.

Biosphere Range

With over 4,000 documented plants, Sikkim is a virtual hothouse and for decades, botanists and plant lovers have been drawn to it. Sikkim's bioshpere ranges roughly over three zones: tropical, temperate and alpine.

Tropical Zone

In the tropical valleys between 250 metres to 1,500 metres, figs, sal and wild bananas consort with a host of bamboo varieties. These forests on the lower hills of south and east Sikkim are caverns of green, strung with sprays of the most amazing orchids and bursts of creamy magnolia.

Beneath the canopy shelters a rich moss and fern life. Covering almost all surfaces – weathered stone, fallen trees and any other debris – the mosses blunt every sharp edge, and colour everything a deep green until they dry to a dull amber. Punctuating these algael undergrowth are the ferns, large and spectacular, in many surreal shapes.

Temperate Zone

The next biospheric zone, stretching from 1,500 metres to 5,000 metres is the reserve of the rhododendron, that hardy flower that sets mountains ablaze when in bloom. In 1849 and 1850, Sir Joseph Hooker's botanical expedition to Sikkim discovered 45 species of rhododendron on the hill slopes of the mountain state. The other trees in these temperate forests are oak, chestnut, maple, birch, alder, magnolia and silver fir.

Alpine Zone

The heights above 5,000 metres are a treeless wilderness, which flare out in beauty when the primulas come to life in summer. Over 40 types of these lilliputian blooms carpet the barren land in mauves, blues and purples. At other times, too, mosses and lichens make intricately beautiful patterns as they spread their sheaths over stones and rockfaces.

Horticulture

Horticulture is one of the major economic activities of the people of Sikkim. Ginger, turmeric and large cardamom are the principal crops, while mandarin orange, guava, and banana are the principal fruits grown in the state. The state government's department of horticulture is deeply involved in motivating and providing technical guidance to local farmers. There is immense potential for developing floriculture into an export-oriented industry.

Tea is also grown extensively in the lower ridges. Sikkimese tea is a connoisseur's delight for its aroma and flavour. There is only one tea estate in Sikkim, Temi Tea Garden, which produces top quality tea. It is spread out on a gentle slope from Tendong Hill in the South district.

Above:*R.Hodgsoni*
Left: A carpet
Owild flowers
Opposite Page from top: *R. Grande*; *R. Thomsoni*; Sikkim's state flower, the orchid *Dendrobium Nobile*; and, a spray of wild orchids

Butterflies

There are over 500 kinds of butterflies in Sikkim and these rainbow creatures add colour to any walk through Sikkim's woods.

Royal Swallow-tail (*Teinopalpus Imperlalls*) or Kaiser-i-hind
This magnificent butterfly can be found in forests between 1,500 metres and 3,000 metres. The female is larger and rarer than the male, but the latter is brighter, with a large yellow area on the upper and undersides of the hind-wings. Its flight is fast and powerful.

Bhutan Glory (*Bhutanitis Ildderdalel Papllionidae*)
As its popular name indicates, this curious looking butterfly is found abundantly in Bhutan and its neighbouring areas, including Sikkim. The body is covered with coarse hairs and for its size the legs are rather short. Its flight is weak and faltering and the wind will take it like a piece of flimsy paper.

Orange Oakleaf (*Kallima inachus Nymphalidae*)
When at rest with its wings closed, this butterfly is indistinguishable from a leaf. The colour and pattern of the undersides is such that it blends with the foliage. This species is on the wing during the rainy season and has a liking for flowering trees and bushes.

Orange Tip (*Hebomoia glaucippe Pieridae Great*)
This is the largest of the Pieridae found in Asia and one of the largest whites in the world. It is very active in the morning.

Malabar Banded Peacock (*Papilio buddha Papllionid)*
This Swallowtail belongs to the species-group *Papilio Palinurus* whose range extends from India through Burma to the Philippines. In marked contrast to the overall metallic mossy green and brilliant green band on the upperside, the underside is a reddish brown, relieved by a few small half-moons on the hindwing. A fast strong flier and prominent throughout the year, except June and July.

Common Map (*Cyrestis thyodamas Nymphalidae*)
The various lines and bands of colour on the wings look like contours on a map, giving this distinctive butterfly its name. Females are slightly larger but paler. It is fond of basking in the sun along the banks of streams and in other damp places.

Birds

The immense variety of Sikkim's avifauna owes much to the natural diversity of the terrain and climate, ranging as it does from the torrid heat of the Terai region, skirting the base of the cool mountain ranges to the arctic cold of its everlasting snows. This makes Sikkim a bird-watcher's paradise, with over 550 species sighted. In fact, close to 50 per cent of the subcontinent's species can be found here.

The range, hence, is enormous, from the tiny Olive Ground Warbler (*Tesia Olivia*) barely 9 cm long, to the huge, Bearded Eagle (*Gypaetus Barbatus*) which has a wingspan of almost two-and-a-half metres.

Perhaps the most beautiful is the monal pheasant called *naurang daphne* by the locals on account of its colourful plumage. It was given its zoological name, *Lophophorous Impejanus*, in honour of Lady Impey, wife of the first Governor General of Bengal who was so taken with the bird that she took it back to England to breed it there.

The lower hills, covered with rich vegetation, shelter some incredible birds, a few of which are migratory. Among the more common birds are the Bulbul, Tit, Thrush, Hoopoe, Cuckoo, Cormorant and Ibis-bill.

An hour's travel up the heights and you can spot Lammergiers, Serpent Eagles, Choughs, and Ravens, while the Satyr Tragopan, Snow Partridge, Snow Cock, Blood Pheasant and Rose Finches inhabit the juniper trees further up the mountains.

Bird-watching in Sikkim is less expensive than in the rest of the Himalayas, largely because the area to be covered is small and the biodiversity rich.

Rufous-bellied Niltava (15 cm)
This sparrow-sized bird has a stunning plumage. Its forehead is black, the sides of its head and back are a deep purplish blue, and its crown, rump, shoulders and neck-patch are a dazzling ultramarine. The rest of the underparts are a bright rufous-orange. The female Niltava is predominantly olive or brown, with a blue patch on each side of the neck and a white one on the lower throat. It prefers the dense undergrowth of forests or bushes by the waterside, hunting for berries and insects. It nests in clumps of moss in crevices of rocks. The Lepchas call it *margong*.

Crested Goshawk (42 cm)
A short-winged hawk, that is dark brown above with its forehead, crown and crest in blackish grey. Its tail has four dark brown bars, while its breast is white, streaked in brown and, thereafter barred with brown. A conspicuous black stripe runs down from chin to breast. The sexes are alike, although the female is larger. A forest dweller, the goshawk is rather sedentary. It perches amidst foliage in the highest branches of a tree, waiting for small ground birds or animals to emerge from the undergrowth, and then swoops down silently. It has a screech for a cry and lays two or three bluish-white eggs in massive (50 cm wide) nests of twigs lined with leaves. Both sexes share the parenting.

Verditer Flycatcher (15 cm)
The male is bluish-green, while the female is duller and greyer. It affects well-wooded country and swoops down on flying insects, capturing them mid-air. It nests in a thick-sided cup of moss under the eaves of houses or in a hole in the wall or embankment or between the exposed roots of a tree. The eggs are usually four and pale pink in colour, but darker at the broad end.

Three-toed Kingfisher (13 cm)
It has a dark purple mantle, an amethyst-blue rump and an orange-yellow underside. It also sports a coral bill and has three-toed legs. The bird is usually found beside shady streams in moist and evergreen forests, feeding on small fish, crustaceans and insects. Its call is a sharp *chichee*. This kingfisher usually nests in a narrow, horizontal tunnel in the earth bank of a *nullah*. It generally lays a cluster of six or seven white eggs.

Blue Chat (15 cm)
The male is slaty blue, with a conspicuous white supercillium, black lores and cheeks. The flanks, throat and breast are all ochre. The female is olive brown above and whitish below. It comes to the damp forests of the mountains to breed and is especially fond of the undergrowth of rhododendron forests. It is an unobtrusive bird, found singly, usually feeding on insects. Its call is a sharp trill (*jerri-jerri-jerri, quick-quick-quick*) on an ascending scale. It nests in a cup of moss on the ground, lined with fur, hair, or grass. It lays blue eggs, usually numbering four, which the female then incubates.

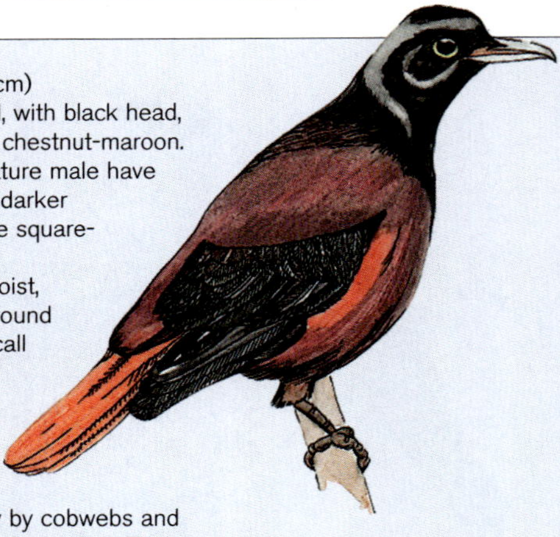

Maroon Oriole (28 cm)
It is a glossy, crimson bird, with black head, neck and wings. Its tail is chestnut-maroon. The female and the immature male have a greyish underbelly with darker streaks. While in flight, the square-cut crimson tail remains diagnostic. It is fond of moist, evergreen glades and is found among the tree-tops. Its call is generally a harsh *kee-ah*, followed by a fluted *pi-lo-lo*. Its nest is a deep cup woven from plant fibre and bound generally by cobwebs and can be found in the fork of a branch. The eggs are pinkish-white, dotted with black or brown. The Lepchas call it *melambok*, while the Nepalese call it *singanee*.

Orange-headed Groundthrush (21 cm)
Its head, neck and belly are rusty chestnut, while the vent and undertail coverts are white. It has a white wing bar. The female's mantle is tinged olive-brown. It is a partial migrant, and comes from the peninsula to the Himalayas to breed. It is found singly or in pairs in damp forests that have plentiful undergrowth. The thrush has a loud, sweet call, but also imitates other birds on occasion. It nests on a pad of moss in the fork of some tree.

Brown Wood Owl (50 cm)
It is chocolate brown in colour, with close, barred underparts and a white supercillium. The face is paler in the hill version and more brownish in the birds found in the plains. The bird has a white patch on throat and tail tipped white. It lives among the dense and moist deciduous forests and is habitually found in pairs. It is very shy, but has the most amazing repertoire of sounds – its call is a musical *tok-tu-hoo*, but it is quite capable of suddenly bursting into a series of eerie shrieks, interspersed with loud snaps of its bill. It is quite non-fastidious in its choice of nesting ground, and can quite happily lay its speckled eggs on a bed of twigs on a rocky shelf, or in the hollow of a tree or even on the ground.

Striated Green Bulbul (20 cm)
It is a small bird with an upstanding brownish-olive crest and its mantle is olive-green, streaked with white. The bird has a yellow ring around the eye, and its wings and tail are olive-brown. The yellow throat and pale yellow outer feathers are its other main characteristics. The male and the female of the species are similar in appearance. It can be found profusely in the evergreen forests pecking at berries and insects. Its call is a loud *pyik-pyik* and it nests in a cup of twigs placed strategically in a bush or in a bamboo cluster. Its eggs are creamy white, with small brown and purple blotches. It is called *senin-plek-pho* by the Lepcha.

Fairy Bluebird (28 cm)
It is a brilliant ultramarine above and a velvety black below. The female differs in being a dull blue-green all over, with blackish spots. It prefers the evergreen and deciduous forests and is often found in fruit trees or berry bushes with others of its kind. It usually lays two olive grey eggs, that have irregular brown blotches all over, and rings round the broad end. Its nest is quite distinctive, being a rough platform of twigs overlaid by a mattress of moss. It can generally be spotted in the fork of a tree.

Sikkim's mightiest mountains are silhouetted against the breaking dawn

Left:
A bejewelled Nepali girl. The Nepalese form the majority of Sikkim's population.
Below:
Bhutia boys try their hands at the cymbals

Ethnic Diversity

Sikkim might seem locked in, but the ranges are punctuated by passes, high but not impenetrable. There are Nathula, Jelepla, Donkiala, Kongrala, where *la*, as in other parts of the Himalayas, means pass. It was through these passes that caravans bearing silk and spices headed for lands beyond the mountains, making Sikkim an important trading stopover and gave it a melange of people as its populace.

The original inhabitants of Sikkim were the mountain people, the Lepchas. They called themselves, the *Rongthub* or the Ravine People or else, the *Mutanchi*, the Beloved People of Mother Earth, and are today a minority community in their own land. They are concentrated in the Dzongu, Penlong and Dikchu valleys of North Sikkim. The late Chogyal of Sikkim, Tashi Namgyal, handed over Dzongu to the Lepchas from his royal estate to serve as a reserve for this fast-dwindling community. The Lepchas are essentially woodsmen who know the ways of the birds and the beasts and possess an extensive zoological and biological nomenclature of their own. Their arts, crafts and songs reflect their deep bond with nature.

A *thanka* depicting the enlightenment of Lord Buddha. For the people of Sikkim, the serene being of the Buddha, radiating compassion, is an eternal beacon.

The Bhutias came over the mountain passes from the Kham province of Tibet. The word Bhutia, in fact, is Nepali for the people of Bhot or Tibet. They are a fun-loving people, and can be often seen holding impromptu soirees on the roadside, rhyming verses and singing folk songs to the accompaniment of the *damney* (string instruments). They are devout Buddhists.

Most Nepali people came in to Sikkim on chain gangs that were brought in to work on the tea plantations and till the fields. They stayed on and today form over 70 per cent of the population. Most are Hindu and follow the usual caste structure with the Bawans or Brahmins at the summit.

History

The history of Sikkim is shrouded in myth. Back in the 8th century, the legendary Buddhist monk Guru Padmasambhava or Guru Rimpoche prophesied that Sikkim would be overrun by Buddhism. This prophecy came to pass in the 17th century, when the Tibetan lama Lhatsun Chempo decided that he must go and 'open the northern gate of *Beyul Demozong*'. He led his disciples to the mountain wall, beyond which lay Sikkim but could find no way to cross the mountain until a vision of the mountain Khang-chen-dzonga showed him the way in.

When Lhatsun Chempo did enter the new country from the north, he found two other lamas, Sempa Chempo and Rigzing Chempo, coming from the west and the south. The three met at a place thereafter known as Yuksam or Place of the Three Wise Ones and decided to launch a hunt for a king. 'Towards the East, it is written,' said Lhatsun reading from Guru Rimpoche's prophecy, 'there is a man named Phuntsog, a descendent of the brave people of Kham from eastern Tibet, and according to the prophecy of the master, we should invite him to join us.'

The prophecy played itself out. The man, Phuntsog, did come out of the east and was duly crowned Chogyal or Great Religious King in 1641. He assumed the family name of Lhatsun Chempo and formed the Namgyal royal house.

A *thanka* from Phensog monastery showing the venerated figure of Guru Padmasambhava or Guru Rimpoche, the patron saint of Sikkim

This story not only personifies the entry of Buddhism into Sikkim, it also strengthens the Lepcha-Bhutia bond that is the cornerstone of Sikkimese culture. For, the man who became king was the descendant of Prince Khye-Bumsa, the Tibetan aristocrat who came into Sikkim childless and was blessed with three sons by the grace of a Lepcha priest, The-Kong Thek. The grateful Bhutia swore a pact of blood-brotherhood with the Lepcha priest, which became symbolic of the Lepcha-Bhutia tie.

Kabi Longstok, about 20 kms from Gangtok, on the way to North Sikkim, is the ancient site of the blood-brotherhood pact between the Bhutias and the Lepchas

The Chogyals ruled without great incidence until the 18th century when neighbouring Nepal began making inroads into Sikkimese territory, much reducing it in size.

However, with the advent of the British into the Himalayan reaches, equations began changing yet again. When the British defeated Nepal in 1817, they returned to Sikkim its southern reaches which had been overrun. But typically the British took their own pound of flesh in the form of suzerainty over the little mountain kingdom.

And typically, too, they lost no opportunity to advance their imperial interests. When the two kingdoms had another round of acrimony in 1834, the British interceded and in return for their exertions had the Chogyal turn over Darjeeling to them.

Another opportunity presented itself fifteen years later. The British superintendent of Darjeeling, Dr Campbell, and the famous naturalist Dr Joseph D Hooker were imprisoned on the orders of Tokhang Namguay, known commonly as Pagla Dewan or the Mad Prime Minister, while on a field trip to Sikkim. The British retaliated by annexing the whole of the Terai regions or the foothill tracts. The subsequent decade that followed was peppered by incidents of insurgency against the British and, in 1860-61, the imperial forces occupied the Sikkim capital of Tumlong.

Nepalese migration into Sikkim was increasing and, over the years, differences deepened between the immigrants and the original inhabitants. In 1880 there was an open clash at Rhenock, in which the British favoured Nepalese interests.

Meanwhile, the British, in a bid to set up trading links to the virgin markets of Tibet, began laying roads through Sikkim. Nervous about British intentions, the Tibetans responded in 1886 by occupying and subsequently fortifying Lingtu, some 12 kms inside Sikkimese territory near Jelepla.

Two years later they attacked the town of Gnathang but were summarily defeated by the British. Alarmed by British advances towards Tibet, China offered a treaty in 1890 under which it ceded all rights over Sikkim in return for control over Tibet.

Claude White, after whom Whitehall in Gangtok is named, was the first British Political Officer with virtual run of Sikkim. This arrangement continued until 1949, when the post was changed to that of Dewan and filled by officers of the Indian Administrative Service.

The ruins of the second capital of the Chogyals at Rabdentse, near Pelling in West Sikkim

The Dewans continued ruling Sikkim in tandem with the Chogyal until 1973 when a pro-democracy movement overran the Sikkim Durbar. Elections were held and Sikkim passed from being an Indian Protectorate to an Associate State with an elected chief minister, while the Chogyal remained the constitutional head. A year later, in May 1975, Sikkim became a full-fledged state of India.

So visit this jewel of India, a land beautiful as few others. Visit it for scenic views and for an adrenalin-pumping dose of adventure.

PEOPLE OF SIKKIM

Sikkim has three main ethnic groups – the Lepchas who were the original inhabitants of the region, the Bhutias who migrated from the eastern part of Tibet starting from the 17th century and the Nepalese who began coming in from the neighbouring kingdom of Nepal in the 19th century. The Nepalese soon outnumbered all other communities and today comprise 70 per cent of Sikkim's population.

For the rest, there are significant numbers of Marwaris, Biharis and Bengalis in the towns of Sikkim who came over after the merger with India and are today occupied mostly in the trading and services sectors. Jorethang and Namchi Bazaar, for instance, are almost preserves of the trading community of Marwaris.

The Lepchas, the original inhabitants of Sikkim, are a simple people, attuned to the rhythms of nature

Lepchas

Before 1642, when the first Chogyal was anointed, the Lepchas did not have a recorded history. They lived a village life under the thrall of local chieftains. Tradition tells of how three lamas from Tibet met at Yuksam in West Sikkim. It was here that they decided to hunt for a king for the land they had come to. They met up with one Phuntsog, and consecrated his accession as the first king of Sikkim.

King Phuntsog Namgyal organised Sikkim into 12 *dzongs* or provinces placing each under a Lepcha *dongpon* or governor. He and the three lamas then set about converting the native Lepchas to Buddhism.

These original inhabitants of Sikkim were of Mongolian stock and followed the Bon faith, worshipping the spirits of mountains, forests and rivers. They were a simple people, at one with the rhythms of nature. Their folk songs and tales tell of their deep bond with their natural surroundings.

The Lepchas have their own script and language. Agriculture is their main occupation and cardamom, cinnamon, paddy and oranges their main crops.

Today many are either Buddhists or Christians. Yet they retain vestigial links with their ancient faith and the *bomthing* or priest is a sought-after man at every Lepcha celebration. The major deities in the Lepcha pantheon include Itbumo, Rom, Ethu Daybu Rum, Kongchen Konglo and Tamsarg Thing.

The Lepchas are today a numerical minority in their own land and are concentrated largely in the Dzongu ethnic reserve in North Sikkim district, surrounded by steep and rocky ridges. They are an aloof people, and do not like to intermarry with the other races.

The Lepchas are expert weavers and cane craftsmen and very handy with the bow and arrow. The traditional Lepcha houses-on-stilts are made of wood or bamboo, without the use of a single nail and are often to be found teetering precariously on the edge of mountain ravines.

Lepcha Festivals

Phang Labsol

(August-September)

The festival in commemoration of Sikkim's resident deity Mt Khang-chen-dzonga. It also traditionally marks the Bhutia-Lepcha brotherhood pact that is the cornerstone of Sikkimese culture. It was born of the Lepcha festival of *Chu* (Mountain) *Rum* (Deity) *Fat* (Propitiation) but has now become a pan-community festival of Sikkim.

The central feature of Phang Labsol celebrations is the Warrior Dance or the Pangtoed (where *pang* means witness and *toed* means praise) which was introduced by the fourth Chogyal, Chador Namgyal. The mountain is represented as a fiery deity in a red mask crowned with skulls and riding a white snow-lion. He is accompanied by two attendant deities, Yabdud and Mzodgna and the dance ends with the three of them riding off on caparisoned white horses.

Loosong or Namsoong

(end December)

When the mountains are covered with snow and the surroundings are white with frost; when the Teesta and the Rangeet turn deep blue and flow downstream, twisting and turning; and when it seems as if the rocks and the riverbeds are smiling, it is time for the Namsoong.

This evocative chant ushers in the Sikkimese New Year. This day is also special to farmers who celebrate it as a harvest festival, offering their crops to the gods and spirits of nature.

Chaang

This local brew is made from fermented millet and is pretty strong and quite heady. The fermented grain is kept at the bottom of a tall bamboo vessel and repeatedly topped with warm water.

Bhutias

The Bhutias came to Sikkim sometime in the 15th century as followers of Prince Khye-Bumsa of Kham in eastern Tibet, who came and settled in the Chumbi Valley. Khye-Bumsa was childless and went to a Lepcha holyman The-Kong-Thek for help. When his wife gave birth to a son thanks to The-Kong-Thek's blessings, Khye-Bumsa entered into a blood-brotherhood pact with the Lepchas at Kabi Longstok, about 20 kms from Gangtok on the road to Mangan. It was later that a descendant of Khye-Bumsa became the first Chogyal of Sikkim.

Bhutias comprise some 10 per cent of Sikkim's total population and are evenly distributed across the state. Tibetan by extraction and Buddhist by faith, they are a people for whom authority flows from the *pipon* or village headman. It is the *pipon* who takes important decisions like when to harvest the crops.

He is also the pivot of the Bhutia traditional legal system, *zamsa*, literally 'public meeting place'. The *pipon*, elected every year, hears grievances and then metes out justice. The Bhutias use the Tibetan script and their language is also a dialect of Tibetan. They are expert at spinning, dyeing and weaving.

Bhutia dress is rather distinctive – the men wear the *pokho*, a loose robe fastened at the neck to one side and gathered at the waist by a sash or *kera*, that is worn with trousers. The women wear the *mokho*, a full-length robe worn over a full-sleeved blouse or *honju* and caught at the waist by a *kera*.

Married women wear a striped apron or *pangdin* over the robe and their jewellery is elaborate with heavy pieces of gold and silver, studded with coral, turquoise and amber. In the far north, Bhutia women smear faces with blackish grease called *kutch* to prevent premature wrinkles caused by the harsh sun and bitter winds.

Bhutia women are quite emancipated, economically and sexually, and polyandry is quite common. If one marries an elder brother, the younger brothers automatically become her husbands.

Buddhist Festivals

Lossar (February-March)
The Tibetan New Year marks the day the Buddha preached the *dharma* to the Devil and is celebrated with much feasting and merrymaking.

Saga Dawa (end May-early June)
Considered thrice-blessed because it marks the birth, the Enlightenment and the *parinirvana* of Lord Buddha. It is marked by devout processions of monks carrying the sacred texts of the *Kangyur* and the *Tengyur* around the town streets.

Drukpa Teshi (August)
This day commemorates the Buddha's first sermon at Sarnath.

Lhabab-Duchen
(end October-November)
It marks the descent of the Buddha from the Heaven of the Thirtythree Gods where he went to pay homage to his dead mother, Queen Mahamaya. He stayed there for three long months, entrancing the gods with His discourses.

All this while, His disciples on earth pined for His return. Finally, Maudgalyayana, the only one with the requisite powers, was sent up to Heaven to prevail upon the gods to allow the Buddha to return to earth. His return is marked as Lhabab-Duchen.

Bhutia monks celebrating the Lossar festival
Overleaf: Monks and a nun at the Phodong monastery

The Bhutias' daily life revolves around Lamaist Buddhism. From lifecycle occasions like births and marriages to the annual events like harvesting and sowing, all major events are ruled by the monk and the monastery. The second son of almost every Bhutia family is dedicated to the faith and becomes a monk.

Becoming a monk

A boy is generally admitted to the monastery after a physical examination between the ages of 8 and 12. His parentage is examined and if he is found of sufficiently pure Tibetan blood, he is admitted to the monastery. He is then handed over to any senior relative he might have in the monastery, along with gifts of tea, food and beer. This tutor then ushers the boy into the Great Assembly Hall by announcing his parentage and asks for the permission of the senior monks to take the boy in as a novice.

As a novice, the boy spends close to three years absorbing the monastic routine, learning to read write and recite the sacred texts. A programme of rigorous instruction then starts, each lama teacher specialises in the *sutras*, *vinaya abhi-dharma*, medicine or *tantra*. These courses are followed by demanding exams and exercises in competitive public debate.

After he has successfully cleared all the exams, the tutor brings the novice to the Great Assembly Hall where the older monks question him vigorously. If they are satisfied with the boy's responses, they allow the boy to be placed under General Rules. For this a sacred *mandala* is drawn in the Great Assemly Hall and all the members of the monastery gather around.

The boy is ceremonially tonsured – in Pemayangtse, this is done with the razor said to have been used by Lama Lhatsun Chempo – and dressed formally in a monk's robes. Accompanied all through by a senior monk known as the 'bride companion', the boy takes the vows that wed him to the Order.

R.B

Dancers from the Nepalese Rai community celebrating the harvest festival with the Sili dance

Nepalese

The Nepalese comprise over 70 per cent of Sikkim's population. They are Hindus and follow the Hindu caste system, beginning with the high-born Bawans or Brahmins. Then come the warrior castes of Chhetris and Thakuris, followed by a host of other castes including Gurungs, Tamangs, Rais, Kamis etc.

The Nepalese came to Sikkim in the middle of the 19th century as [illegible] labour for the vast farms and plantations of the Bhutia and Lepcha landowners, as well as for the British tea plantations near Darjeeling. Hill farming was a technique the Nepalese were familiar with, and they introduced the productive method of terrace farming to the mountainous regions of Sikkim, earning themselves a place in the state's history. In fact, the name Sikkim comes from *Sukhim*, Nepali for 'New Home'.

The majority of Nepalese are Hindus, many leaning towards the Tantric school, and the sacrifice-based cult of the Mother Goddess is popular. Consequently, the *jhakris* or shamans have plenty to do, exorcising spirits and casting spells for any number of problems and predicaments. Nepali, written in the Devanagri script, is one of the main languages of Sikkim, together with Bhutia and Lepcha. English is commonly understood, especially in towns and among those involved in tourism.

Nepali Festivals

Maghe Sankranti (January)
It corresponds to the Indian festival of Makara Sankranti and is marked by people bathing in holy rivers.

Dasain (September-October)
This is the Nepali version of the nine-day long Durga Puja. The first day of the festival, called *Ghatasthapana,* sees the installation of the *kalash* or sacred vessel in the family *puja* room. Prayers are chanted to invoke the Goddess Durga and persuade her to alight on the rim of the *kalash*, even if it be for as long as a mustard seed can balance on the horn of a cow.

The prayers and celebrations continue until the seventh day, called *Phulpatti* or Flower Day when the goddess is propitiated with flowers. The eighth day or *Ashtami* is the most sacred, and the orthodox fast in preparation for *Kalratri* or Black Night when animal sacrifices are made to represent the demon slain by Goddess Durga. The tenth day is Vijaya Dashami or *Tika* when the triumph of evil is commemorated by anointing each other's foreheads with the sacred mark or *tika.*

Tihar (November)
A five-day festival, its third day corresponds to the Indian festival of Diwali. The first day is celebrated as *kag tihar* or the festival of crows, when delicacies are prepared and fed to the crows; then comes *kukoor tihar* or the festival of dogs; then *gai tihar*, whose evening is devoted to the celebration of the Goddess Lakshmi and houses are decorated with lights; the following day is *goru* (ox) *tihar*. The last day is *Bhai Tika*, when sisters mark their brothers' foreheads with *tikas.*

Nepali Dances

Sangini
It is a dance with lamps, performed during *Teej* by the married women of the Bahun community and it enacts a married daughter's visit to her parents. The hardships she faces in her in-laws' home are recalled in the dance.

Chabrung or Kaylang
A dance of the Limboo community in praise of the wonders of nature, it is performed at all auspicious occasions, especially weddings.

Mahakali and Lakhey
Masked dances of the Newars, these symbolise the triumph of good over evil. The Mahakali dance depicts the defeat the Goddess Mahakali and her eight associates inflicted on the demons, while the Lakhey is more celebratory in form.

Sakewa Sili
A harvest dance of the Rai community it offers thanks to the earth for her bounty.

Chandi Puja
The Sunuwar community's most revered deity is the Goddess Chandi and the Baisakhi Shukla Purnima sees them take to the streets in her honour. This is also when they dance the Chandi to the rhythm of eight different types of drums.

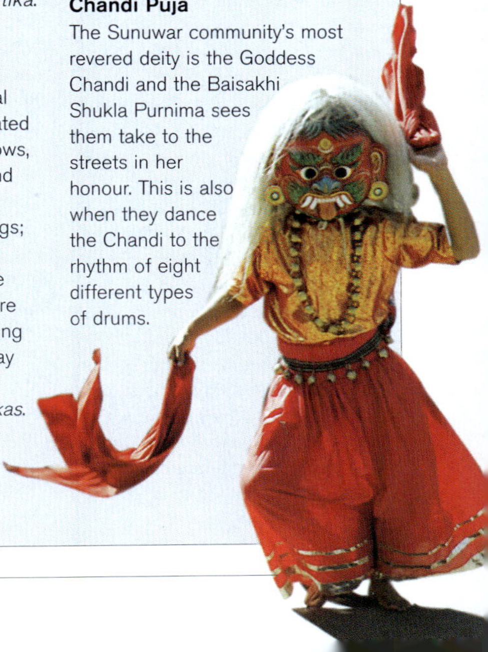

Famous Sons of Sikkim

Baichung Bhutia

One of contemporary Sikkim's most famous sons is the footballer Baichung Bhutia. Born in the village of Tinikitam near Gangtok in December 1976, he grew up in a state that loves soccer. 'Growing up, I watched a lot of local football and like everyone else in India, had local heroes,' Baichung said in an interview once. 'I always used to watch the World Cup on TV, and I really admired Maradona.'

His skill in the Indian junior league Subroto Cup brought him into the limelight in 1992 and he was picked up by a series of leading national clubs. At 21, he was the youngest player to captain East Bengal, one of the two premier clubs of football-crazy Kolkata. Fresh and fearless, he became an instant hero of the crowds.

A few years later, he went to England for trials with the first division club Aston Villa. He did not make the grade there but was snapped up by the second division Bury FC in 2000, becoming the first Indian to play in the English football league. 'I found it very difficult to start with' he said sometime ago. 'I was used to playing in India where obviously the temperature is very high, so the style of play is totally different – a lot slower. As well as the fast pace of the game, I had to get used to the physical aspect of English football, which is a lot tougher than what I was used to back home.'

He is still with Bury, but comes back to India intermittently to play for the national team. He has since returned to Sikkim a couple of times and even participated in football coaching camps for school boys.

Danny Denzongpa

One of the most famous villains of Hindi cinema was born and brought up in Yuksam in West Sikkim. Danny Denzongpa, born Tshering Pintso Denzongpa and rechristened by fellow-actor Jaya Bachchan, left Sikkim for Bombay in 1970 to join the film industry, but has kept alive his roots. Today, Denzongpa runs a tourist resort in his hometown and also has an interest in Sikkim's leading brewery, which turns out the popular Dansberg brand of beer. Denzongpa is the celluloid villain who inspires terror in his audiences with the merest narrowing of his eyes. The Sikkim-born actor made his debut in *Zaroorat* in 1971 and followed this with memorably villainous performances in a string of hits over three decades.

Denzongpa is deeply involved with life in his home state. In fact, when the Sikkim government proposed in the mid-1990s to dam the Rathong Chu, thus endangering the biodiversity in the Khang-chen-dzonga National Park, Denzongpa led a people's protest against the project and forced the authorities to backtrack.

A dancer at the Phang Labsol festivities. Although of Lepcha origin, Phang Labsol is also celebrated by the Bhutias

LAND OF PADMASAMBHAV

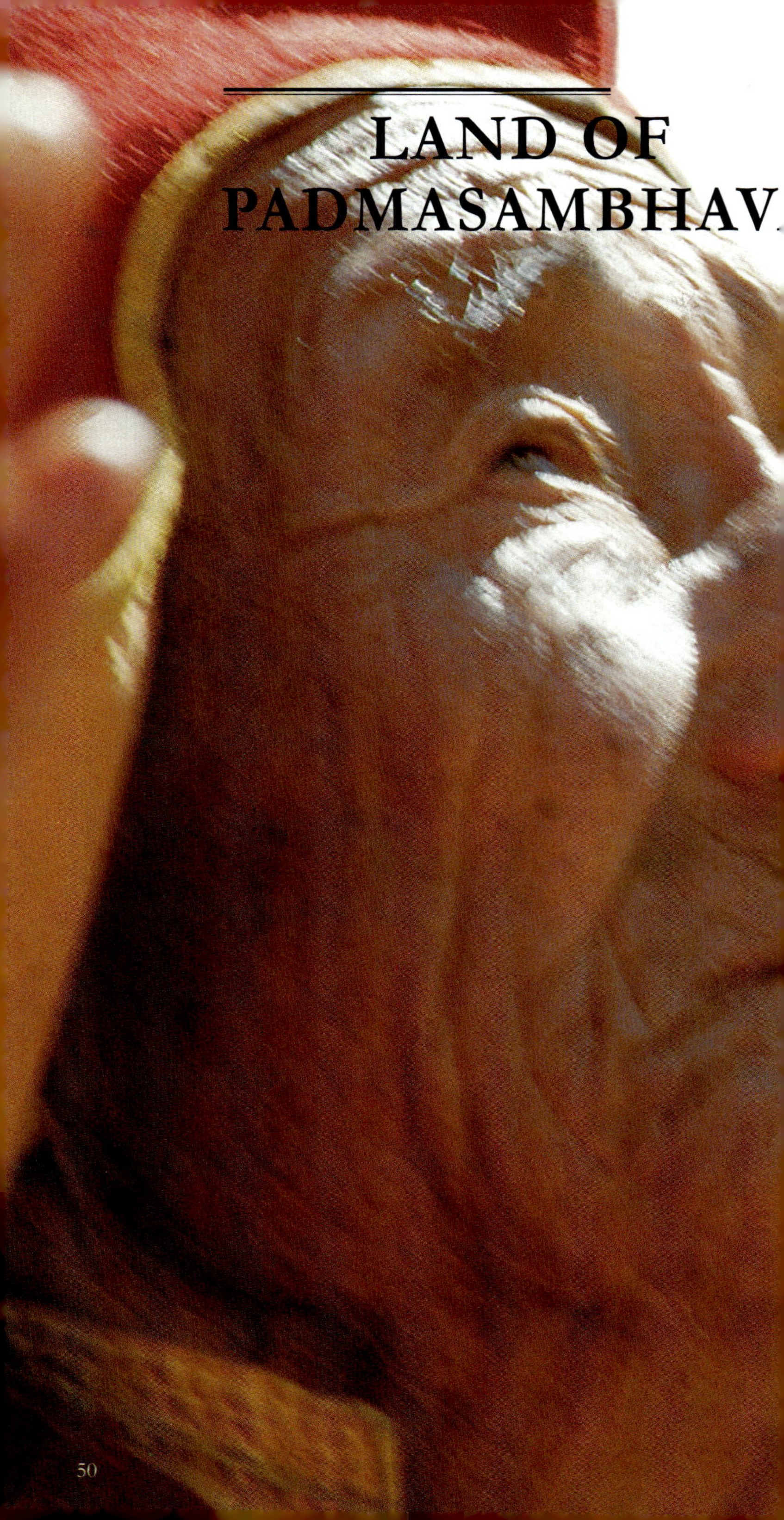

Buddhism in Sikkim

'Om Mani Padme Hum.'
Hail, Jewel in the Lotus.

In the highest reaches of Sikkim, cradled in the crook of the Khang-chen-dzonga, are walls of stone etched with these sacred six syllables. It is the submission of the devout in a land so barren and bare that the only offering is stone.

Buddhism is a tangible presence in Sikkim, its symbols seen everywhere. White prayer flags fluttering in the wind; boy-monks in maroon scampering on the streets; and gaudily painted monasteries splendid in their isolation.

Although Buddhism is no longer the religion of the majority of Sikkimese, it is, even today, the inspiring force behind the people's lives, a deep and abiding faith that permeates every cultural aspect.

An image of the Buddha enshrined in Enchey *gompa* in Gangtok
Opposite Page: Lhatsun Chempo

Coming of Buddhism

Before the coming of Buddhism, the indigenous people of Sikkim followed the Bon religion, an animistic, shamanistic religion centred on rural communities. Buddhism came to Sikkim from Tibet through the divine agency of Guru Padmasambhava ('Lotus Born'), also known as Guru Rimpoche, who, in the 8th century, prophesied that Buddhism would overrun Sikkim.

The prophecy came true in the 17th century, with the coming of the three lamas. One of the lamas was the venerated Lhatsun Chempo, who formally introduced Buddhism to Sikkim. Born in 1595 AD, Lhatsun Chempo was a native of Kongbu in Tibet. He travelled from monastery to monastery in Tibet until he arrived in Lhasa in 1648. Here he attracted the attention of Grand Lama Gyalwa Ngak Wang, who was to become the first Dalai Lama.

From Lhasa, armed with the Grand Lama's blessings, he set about seeking a way into Sikkim. Unable to find a path through the mountains, Lhatsun Chempo is said to have used his mystical powers to fly to the top of Mt Kabru, from where he surveyed the landscape until he found the way into the hidden valley.

Once in Sikkim, he met two other Lamas, Sempa Chempo and Rigzing Chempo, who had entered Sikkim from the west and the south respectively. The place where the three converged was thenceforth called Yuksam or Place of the Three Wise Ones. It was here that they decided to seek out a monarch for Sikkim and where they crowned Phuntsog Namgyal as Chogyal.

After the coronation, Lama Lhatsun Chempo concentrated on spreading the teachings of the Buddha. He set up several monasteries or *gompas* across the country, which spearheaded the diffusion of the religion. Lhatsun Chempo is represented in Buddhist art as seated on a leopard skin mat, almost naked, and with his right leg dangling down. He is blue-skinned, a chaplet of skulls adorns his brow and in his left hand he carries a skull-cup filled with blood.

Vajra

The *Vajra* or thunderbolt, from which Vajrayana Buddhism takes its name, is the symbol of unlimited power. The *vajra* is always held with the bell or *dribul*, and together they signify method and knowledge as being the path to *nirvana*.

Vajrayana

Sikkimese Buddhists today follow the Vajrayana school, an offshoot of Mahayana Buddhism that owes much to Tantric Hinduism. Vajrayana is a system of esoteric Buddhism that includes popular magico-religious idiom such as spirits, spells, and folklore cosmology.

Vajrayana Buddhism centres on the three pivots of *mantra* or sacred chants, *mudra* or symbolic gestures and *mandala* or cosmic diagrams. The inclusion of liturgical rites and the worship of the Taras or female energies personified as consorts of the Bodhisattavas are other characteristics of Vajrayana Buddhism. This school also stresses the importance of the *guru* or teacher, who guides the disciple in his search for spiritual powers that will allow him to unite with the Supreme.

Guru Rimpoche

Guru Padmasambhava ('Lotus Born') was also known as Guru Rimpoche. He came to Tibet by the effort of King Thi Sung Dewtson (AD 740-786), whose mother was a Chinese princess (generally symbolised in Tibetan iconography as the White Tara) who greatly influenced him in favour of Buddhism. Seeking to spread the word of the Lord, he sent to India for books and teachers and initiated the translation into Tibetan of Sanskrit and Chinese texts.

Soon after his accession, he decided to give Tibet its first monastery at Samye. However, he found his efforts constantly thwarted by earthquakes, generally thought to be the work of the local pre-Buddhist demon-deities angered by the implantation of Buddhism on their land.

On the advice of the Indian monk, Shantarakshita, the King sent to Nalanda for the great monk, Padmasambhava. He arrived in Tibet by way of Nepal in AD 747 with two wives and a host of disciples.

At Samye, Guru Padmasambhava pacified deities and also created a sacred Buddhist space by drawing a *mandala*. On this mandala was laid the foundation of the Samye monastery, which itself was in the shape of a circular *mandala*.

A *yab-yum* mural symbolising the union of male wisdom and female compassion

The Vajrayana pantheon comprises the Adi Buddha (Supreme Buddha) and the five Jina or Conqueror Buddhas who emerged from His meditations. These are Vero Tsana, the central Jina, and the four Jinas associated with the cardinal directions – Amoghasiddhi, Ratnasambhava, Aksobhya and Amitabha.

The devotee invokes them through *mantras*, mentally encloses them within *mandalas* and identifies himself with them through meditation. Many are represented as embracing their female counterparts, symbolising the *yab-yum* or the union of male wisdom and female compassion, which is the essence of the Bodhisattava ideal.

Buddhist Sects

There are two important sects of Buddhism in Sikkim, Nyingmapa and Kagyupa.

Nyingmapa

Nyingma is the older sect, more akin to the pre-Buddhist indigenous practices, and celibacy and abstinence are rarely practised. Pemayangtse is the seat of the Nyingmapa in Sikkim and the Samye monastery of Tibet is its oldest institution.

Historically, Nyingmapa is the only school of Tibetan Buddhism that traces its origin directly to Guru Padmasambhava and his principal disciples to whom he imparted lessons in the highest class of *tantra*. These first Tibetan adepts are renowned for their spiritual accomplishments; for example, Namkhe Nyingpo is known for his feat of travelling on beams of light, Khandro Yeshe Tsogyal for reviving the dead, Vero Tsana for his intuition, Nanam Yeshe for his ability to soar in the sky and Kawa Peltseg for reading the thoughts of others.

However, seeing that time was inappropriate for many of the other teachings he had to reveal, Guru Rimpoche is said to have hidden hundreds of scriptures, images and ritual articles, with instructions for their revelation for the benefit of future generations. Subsequently, several hundred *tertons* or diviners have revealed these treasures and taught them to their disciples. So, besides the tantric teachings, it is these lineages of revealed teachings or *terma* that are distinguished as the Nyingma doctrine. It remained the only form of Buddhism in Tibet for two centuries. Then native Bon religion struck back and Buddhists were viciously persecuted in the 9th century leading to the decline of the new creed.

The Nyingma school is also distinguished by the emphasis it places on the life of the layman as a valid path toward realisation, as well as its acceptance of an equal role for woman in transmitting the *Dharma*.

A funeral procession at Phensog monastery

Little boy monks at the Rumtek seminary, learning the scriptures by rote

Kagyupa

The Kagyu school, on the other hand, is the reformed sect that was formed sometime in the 11th century and is headquartered at the Rumtek Dharmachakra Centre today. The Kagyu lineage traces its origins to the great Tibetan sage, Marpa (1012-1099) who studied *tantra* at the feet of the learned monk Naropa in India and returned to Tibet to pass on the teachings to several scholars, notable among them being Milarepa (1040-1123), the most celebrated of Tibetan *yogis*.

The teachings, passed down through the ages from one adept to another, crystallised into the Dagpo Kagyu tradition, the mother Kagyu lineage, of which the Karma Kagyus are the most well-known.

Other Tibetan Buddhist Sects

Sakyapa

The venerated Indian monk, Atisa, travelled to Tibet in 1042 and his teachings led to a renewal of the Buddhist faith in that land. The century before had seen Buddhism mutate into a magical, quasi-shamanistic, tantric creed. Atisa's disciples stressed the *Vinaya* orthodoxy and the reformed sect that emerged was the Sakya.

Gelugpa

Also known as the Yellow Hat sect, it came into being in the early 15th century from the teachings of Tsongkhapa (1358-1419) and grew into the most powerful sect of Tibetan Buddhism, including as it did the lineages of both the Dalai Lama and the Panchen Lama.

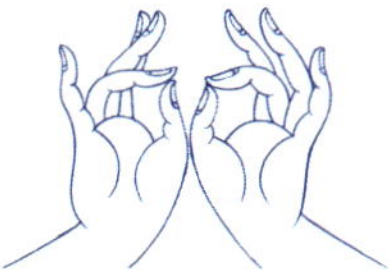

Tashi-Tyagi

These are the eight auspicious signs of Vajrayana Buddhism and can be found on *thankas* and paintings, on buildings and even furniture.

They include the *dug* or golden umbrella that symbolises the Buddha

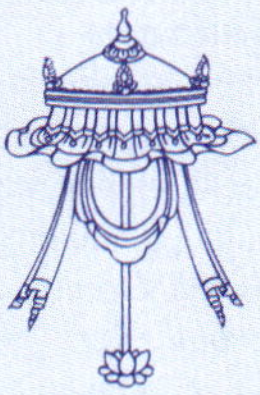

The *gyaltsen* or banner of victory of good over evil

The *sernya* or golden fish symbolising rebirth

The *dhungkar* or conchshell symbolising the reverberating sound of *dharma*

The *bhumpa* or vase that symbolises unlimited wealth, health and longevity

The *pema* or lotus symbolising the ultimate goal of enlightenment

The *palbheu* or the knot of eternity

The *choekyi khorlo* or *dharmachakra*, the symbol of the Buddha's teachings.

Medongs

These are stone walls faced with blocks etched with the six-syllabled *mantra*, *Om Mani Padme Hum.* It is considered a pious act to add to these *medongs*, so masons are generally retained by monasteries to add blocks to the walls at the order and expense of the devout.

Gompas

The *gompa*, literally a Solitary Place, is the pivot of Lamaist Buddhism. Isolation was seen as an aide to meditation, so monasteries were built at remote locations. The *gompa* had its origins in the spartan *viharas* or residences that the *bhikshus* hewed out of rock during the Buddha's time. Spread of the *dharma* and increased patronage by both royalty and the laity led to the monasteries being enlarged on such a magnificent scale that *gompas* like Tashiding became large monastic establishments.

A scriptural couplet decrees that a *gompa* should be built with its 'Back to the hill-rock/ And front to the tarn'. So, most Sikkimese *gompas* are usually found on the long axis of a hill, facing eastward, with a lake in the front. Lining the approaches of most monasteries are rows upon rows of fluttering prayer flags, lichen-covered *chortens* and *medong* walls.

Prayer Flags

Fluttering prayer flags are an abiding part of the Sikkimese landscape. The flags, usually in the white of purity, carry the prayers of the faithful on the wings of the wind. Prayer flags are of four types: *Lungta* or the Wind Horse type are essentially strips of cloth with a picture of a horse, bearing a jewel on its back; the *Chopen* or Luck Flags are oblong pieces of cloth tied to tree branches; the *Gyaltsen* or Victory Banner has holy text inscribed on it; and the *Glan Po Stob Ryyas* or the Vast Lucky Flag has a symbol of crossed dorjees or thunderbolts and a peacock.

The richly-decorated exterior of Lachung *gompa* in North Sikkim

Once at the *gompa*, the pilgrim enters the *dukhang* or the assembly hall, passing through a portico that connects the sacred environs to the outside world. Reach Enchey monastery in Gangtok any time of the day, and you will find the monks lining the *dukhang*, engaged in a number of ritual activities, often the head lama himself at the heart of the gathering. And everywhere there is an overwhelming smell of burning incense.

The *lhakhang*, literally God's Room, is the most sacred area of the *gompa*. Here is enshrined the central image of the deity, as well as the attendant images, with butter lamps burning before them. The *lhakhang* walls are decorated with murals and *thankas* and only selected monks are allowed entry – and that, too, after going through elaborate purifying rituals.

Community kitchens aglitter with large utensils, larders choked with barley and butter, and rooms full of musical instruments are the other buildings within a *gompa*.

All *gompas* also have libraries stocked with xylographs of the *Kangyur* and *Tengyur*. These two sacred books are carried out in processions on special festivals. There are also separate halls for teaching *tantra* and *sutra*.

Given Sikkim's mountain terrain, the courtyard is generally the only open space in the *gompa* and this comes to life during the annual *chaam* festival.

Gompa interiors are breathtaking with their store of *thankas*, *mandalas*, innumerable images of the Buddha, musical instruments, masks, *vajras*, bells and beads, and butter sculptures. Cast images in bronze are commonly found in the niches of the *lhakhang* and the *dukhang*. Crafted with great precision, each element of these small images has a tale to tell, a tale understood by every layman in the Buddhist universe. The Buddha, the Bodhisattavas and the Taras are the most popular and most venerated subjects of these images.

Chortens

Literally, receptacles for offerings, *chortens* are solid conical structures originally intended as relic-holders, but now more often erected as cenotaphs.

They are abundant around monasteries, rising white from the surrounding green. Some devotees carry small replicas of *chortens* made of metal for meditation. The *chorten* has five parts in a definite proportion representing the five elements of air, water, earth, fire and ether. It consists of a solid hemisphere, the true relic-holder mounted on a block. This, in turn, is surmounted by a narrow neck that culminates in a lotus-leafed basin, bearing an elongated disc. It must be circumambulated keeping it to the right of the devotee.

Left:
An enthralled audience watches the annual *chaam* in Lachung monastery

Another category of statues are the *yab-yum* images that show the Bodhisattavas and the Taras in poses suggestive of a sexual element. In Vajrayana philosophy, however, these signify the union of the 'male' element of wisdom and the 'female' one of compassion.

Lamas, who follow a hierarchic system, perform all ritualistic ceremonies at a *gompa*. The order is generally composed of non-celibate monks and nuns, called *anneys*.

Wheel of Life

The most significant of Buddhist symbols, it is found on the entrances of monasteries as well as on *thankas*. Its circular form symbolises ceaseless worldly existence. The wheel is held in the clutches of a monster who grips it with his claws and his teeth, a representation of how mankind is gripped by materialism.

The centre of the wheel contains a picture of a cock (symbolising lust and desire), a snake (a symbol of anger) and a pig (representing ignorance). As the ills represented by these animals are the root cause of all suffering in the world, they also form the hub of the Wheel of Life.

The middle circle depicts the five worlds delineated by the Buddha, of which the upper two worlds represent the heavenly and the human worlds, while the lower three are the worlds of animals, ghosts and hell. The rim between the hub and the middle circle is drawn half in black and half white, symbolising the good and evil deeds that make up life. The outermost circle shows the 12 phases of life.

Thankas

A *thanka* is a hand-painted religious painting drawn on fabric. Part of Buddhist iconography, the art of *thanka* painting originated in India and travelled to Tibet in the 8th century. Today, *thankas* are hung in *gompas* throughout the Himalayan region, from Arunachal Pradesh in the east, through Sikkim and Bhutan to Ladakh and Tibet, and are used for ritual purposes or as aids for meditation.

The *thanka* painter is generally regarded as a holy person, his tools the instruments of divinity and the creation of a *thanka* is more an act of devotion than an art exercise. The painter rigorously follows the rules of scale and perception laid down in the Buddhist scriptures for he is aware that, without this, the *thanka* will not be able to host the Divine Spirit. As in the case of Hindu *murtis* or idols, an elaborate ritual breathing the Divine Spirit into it consecrates the completed *thanka*.

The painter stretches the fabric tight across a wooden frame and drenches it with glue. He then runs a piece of glass over it to smooth the surface. He checks the tactility of the cloth by striking a finger against it. If it pings, the fabric is ready to be painted upon. He begins his devotional art by drawing a line diagonally across the cloth. He outlines the iconographic figures with charcoal before filling the surface with traditional motifs, designs and colours.

The themes of the *thankas* relate to the Buddha and his life, as well as to the lives of the Bodhisattavas, the Taras, the great saints and Buddhist masters. They also depict mystical concepts like the Wheel of Life, the Tashi Tagyi and *mandalas*. Some *thankas* depicting these abstract themes are on permanent display at the Institute of Tibetology in Gangtok.

There are rigid iconographical proportions to be followed in painting a figure-centric *thanka*: for instance, the depicted saint must have a perfectly-proportioned body, be seated in a typical pose, and must display 'mild' gestures. Guru Rimpoche is particularly popular in Sikkim and he is always portrayed seated on a cloud, with a *dorje* or thunderbolt in his right hand. The guardian deities or the *srung-ma*, the tutelary deities or *yidam*, and the demoniacal beings, on the other hand, are all depicted with exaggerated features like swollen arms and protruding teeth. They are also painted in dark colours like red and black *thankas* from the period before 8th century were simple ones, with a single deity ensconced against a plain background.
Over the centuries, ornate backdrops like waterfalls and elaborate gardens were added to create an effect of paradise.

Pemayangtse monastery, for instance, has a stunning collection of *thankas* depicting the tales from the *Jatakas*.

The devout commission a *thanka* for various purposes – to pray for a long life, to serve as a good luck charm, to pray for the favourable rebirth of a person recently dead or simply to accumulate religious merit. *Thankas* also serve as models on which the devotee can reflect to improve his spiritual wellbeing. So, a novice monk worships a *yidam* or personal deity and models his personality on that deity. *Thankas* are carried out in elaborate processions during festivals like the Saga Dawa and Lossar.

Thankas depicting the wisdom tree, with its diseased and healthy branches, are used to teach medicine to the *amchis* or medicine men at Sangacholing monastery.

An art form closely allied to the *thankas* is the making of *gos-sku* or giant, applique banners of silk. The slopes of hills are cleared to unveil the massive *gos-sku* during festivals. For instance, people come from afar to see the famous *gos-sku* in Tashiding monastery as it is believed that the mere sight of it confers liberation.

A *thanka* depicting Mayadevi giving birth to prince Siddharth

Chaam

Sikkim's famous mask dances are simply spectacular. Performed on festivals in *gompa* courtyards by both lamas and laymen, these dances demonstrate the importance of ritual in Sikkim's culture.

The *chaams* might tell different stories, but thematically they all deal with the triumph of good over evil. The dancers wear fearful dragon, animal and bird masks, dress in richly-brocaded costumes and tread the measure to the sound of cymbals and trumpets.

The *chaam* starts with the heraldic call of *kangling* trumpets from within the *gompa*. The deep notes of the *radong* copper horns from outside the *gompa* answer it. Cymbals, drums, and gongs sound in rhythmic unison the start of the dance. Richly attired dancers file into the monastery courtyard and even as they swirl in rich colour, incense-bearers circulate among the audience, purifying the atmosphere.

The actual dance drama then begins. The central figure of most *chaams* is Mahakala, the Grand Lord who commands the rhythms of Time or *kaal*.

In the Loosong or New Year *chaam*, for instance, Mahakala is worshipped in elaborate detail on the first of the two-day celebrations.

The legend about the origin of *chaam* tells of a 9th century king called Ral Pa Chen. A devout Buddhist, he had important scriptures translated into Tibetan and endowed many monasteries.

Watching a *chaam* is an overwhelming experience. Masked dancers attired in silk-and-brocade robes and bizarre masks perform intricate dances to the accompaniment of trumpets and cymbals.

However, there was a malevolent force at work in his kingdom in the form of his brother Lang Darma. This baleful man had his brother murdered and grabbed the throne himself.

And, as king, he set about destroying the faith: He desecrated temples and monasteries, burned sacred books and scriptures and persecuted lamas.

This sacrilege continued until he was assassinated by Lama Pal Dorjee. The lama came to court with a dance troupe, disguised as a devil dancer. He caught the king's attention with his skilful dancing and when the king beckoned him closer, whipped out a bow and arrow hidden up his sleeve and killed him. Dorjee escaped on a black pony, with the king's guard in hot pursuit. But he eluded capture by plunging into the Kyi-chu River, pony and all. When he emerged on the other bank, the pony was snow-white and this miraculous transformation fooled the pursuers.

The demon-god Mahakala is the central figure of all *chaam* dances. His black mask heightens his fearsome presence, his lips drawn back in a snarl, and his brow wreathed in skulls.

GOMPAS OF SIKKIM

Sikkim's *gompas* are among the state's biggest attractions. Dotted all across the mountain state, the monasteries with their distinctive architecture and exotic relics and icons draw tourists in large numbers. While Pemayangtse, Rumtek and the Tsukhlakhang in Gangtok remain fixtures on most itineraries, those seeking the splendid and the picturesque must also try and visit the lesser known *gompas* like Phodong, Lachung and Tashiding.

The Dharmachakra Centre at Rumtek is the largest and most prosperous monastery of Sikkim
Opposite Page: A Tara statue from Rumtek

Rumtek

The road from Gangtok winds through green paddy terraces for 24 kms before arriving at this seat of the Kagyu or the Black Hat sect, situated on the hill facing Gangtok. It was built in 1959 by the 16th Gyalwa Karmapa. It is a replica of the Tsurphu monastery, his seat in the Kham region of Tibet, which he had to abandon when Chinese forces occupied Tibet. He fled over the mountains to Sikkim, carrying Tsurphu's treasures with him.

The Kagyu sect originated in Tibet in the 11th century. According to legend, the first Karmapa spent many years meditating in a cave. One day, he was visited by ten thousand spirits each offering him a strand of hair.

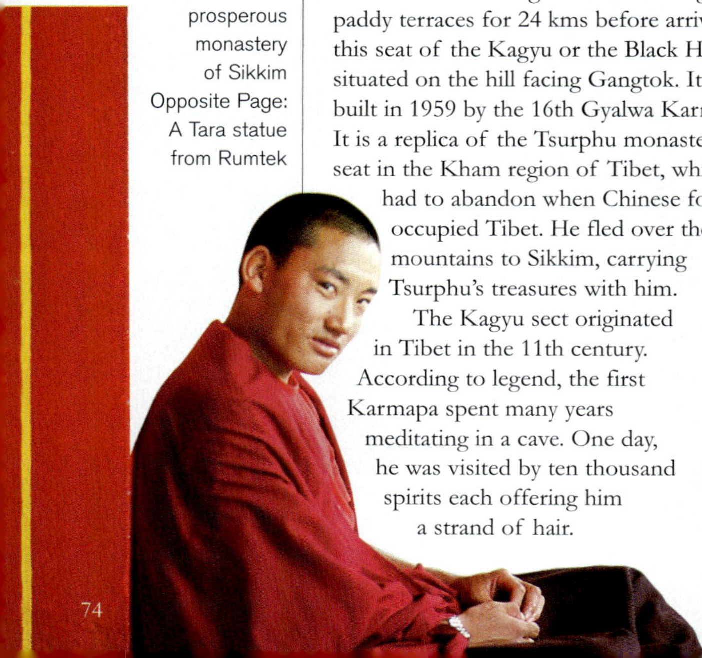

These were woven into a black hat that came to be passed down from Karmapa to Karmapa, to be worn at ceremonial occasions. It is also said that the magical hat will vanish unless it is kept in a box or otherwise held down while worn. It is this very same hat that is said to lie in Rumtek monastery.

Rumtek, the largest monastery in Sikkim, is a fine example of Tibetan architecture. The three-storied monastery has a great assembly hall on the ground floor, where little tables line the walls. On the first floor are the living quarters of the last Karmapa, while the top floor has a small *stupa*.

There is a marked air of prosperity about the Rumtek *gompa*. As the seat of the Kagyupa, the Dharmachakra Centre is quite well provided for. In fact, a recent evaluation of its assets has put the figure at billions of rupees.

The Rumtek seminary is also one of the most popular ones and a morning visit will find the courtyard abuzz with little boy monks preparing for their lessons or generally releasing pent-up energies. Rumtek's main celebration is held on the 10th day of the 5th month of the Tibetan calendar, roughly contiguous with June. This is when the Tse-Chu *chaam* dance is held in a burst of colour.

The great assembly hall of the Rumtek monastery is a treasure trove of statues, *thankas* and silk banners

Pemayangtse

The monastery named for the Sublime Perfect Lotus is situated 112 kms west of Gangtok and, from a height of 2137 metres, commands a magnificent view of the mighty Khang-chen-dzonga. The monastery was built in 1705 and is the second oldest, as well as second most important monastery of Sikkim, being the seat of the Nyingma sect. It retains its reputation for the celibacy and pure pedigree of its monks. In fact, it was set up primarily for the pure-blooded or *ta-song* Bhutia men and the honour of anointing a newly-crowned sovereign with holy water was always reserved for the head lama of Pemayangtse.

Pemayangtse *gompa* is the seat of the Nyingma sect and one of the most revered monasteries in Sikkim

Situated 6 kms from the town of Gyaltshing, the district headquarters of West Sikkim, the monastery houses several priceless religious idols and icons. Its interiors are covered with brightly-painted murals of the Tibetan Buddhism pantheon. But the highlight of Pemayangtse is the elaborately-carved wooden sculpture on the top floor of *Sang-tok-palri*, the heavenly abode of Guru Padmasambhava or Guru Rimpoche.

Its secluded location away from the main road and its determined austerity give the Pemayangtse *gompa* an anachronistic feel. It seems caught within a time warp, somewhere in the middle ages, completely untouched by the 21st century. So, when the jeeps vroom in, bringing their afternoon loads of tourists, it seems like an intrusion.

Pemayangtse is also one of the most revered monasteries of Sikkim and the tourist inflow has not deterred the pilgrims. In fact, just outside the *gompa* lie the community kitchens, where women and children are almost always busy grinding rice to make *jerros*. These crisp, filigreed rice cakes are then distributed to the many pilgrims who come to worship at the *gompa* each day.

The main festival of Pemayangtse is held on the 28th and 29th days of the 12th month of the Tibetan calendar, corresponding roughly to the month of February.

Tashiding

A monastery of the Nyingma sect, Tashiding is in West Sikkim, situated some 40 kms from Gyaltshing via Legship, and forms a beautiful sight framed against the mighty Khang-chen-dzonga. Tashiding was built in 1716 by Pedi Wangmo, half-sister of Chogyal Chador Namgyal, on the spot where an arrow supposedly shot off by Guru Rimpoche landed.

It is located on a secluded hilltop, surrounded by forests and between two rivers, the Rathong and the Rangeet. The holiest *chorten* of Sikkim, the Thongwa Randol, is situated here, and it is said that a mere glimpse of this *chorten* is enough to cleanse all sins.

The main festival here is the Bumchu, held on the midnight of the 14th-15th of the first Tibetan month. Lore has it that, some three hundred years ago, a holy man, Gandak Chempo, blessed a little water after chanting *Om Mani Padme Hum* five billion times. This consecrated water was preserved in a jar at Tashiding. At every Bumchu festival, this water is poured into 21 small jars and used for divining the fortunes of Sikkim.

Prayer Wheels

The prayer wheels are the constant reminder of the presence of the Buddha and a simple aid to meditation. Lamas and nuns with prayer wheels are a familiar sight in the Lepcha and Bhutia villages of Sikkim. They go from one valley to the other, rotating the prayer wheel in an act of unstinted devotion.

A mural painted on the walls of the Pemayangtse monastery

Dos and Don'ts

- Please be decently attired – no shorts or short dresses.
- Please move around the *gompa* in a clockwise direction
- Please refrain from smoking
- Remember to take off your shoes before entering the monastery
- Do not sit on the benches inside the monastery; they are meant strictly for the monks.

Tholung

Aptly named The Stony Valley, this is the most inaccessible of all Sikkim's monasteries and can be accessed only after a three-day trek from Mangan in North Sikkim, through dense forests and across steep ridges. But the effort is well worth the while, for the monastery houses many antique treasures like *thankas*, horse saddles and thigh-bone trumpets. It is said that Lhatsun Chempo had a premonition about the Gorkha invasion and sent the most precious of the sacred objects of various monasteries to Tholung for safekeeping. A brass *chorten* in the monastery is said to contain the ashes of Lhatsun Chempo. All the other relics are kept in 13 sealed boxes that are opened for the public once every three years.

Mandalas

These are ritual diagrams used in *tantra* and Buddhist *dharma*, each being a symbolic miniature universe that serves as a focus for meditation. Made of sand, sawdust or coloured powder, the *mandala* is ritually destroyed after its purpose has been served, thus signifying the spirit of detachment.

The theory and techniques of drawing a *mandala* have been forged in antiquity and are passed down from *guru* or master to disciple. At the centre of the *mandala* lies the sacred Mt Meru, the mythical axis of the universe. This symbolic territory is then peopled with circles, lotus flowers, and squares.

A *mandala* also represents a sacred mansion or temple, at the heart of which resides a deity. So lines are sketched with sand, rice powder or paint and ink, and inscribed with auspicious symbols and *mantras*. *Mandalas* drawn on paper are often folded and carried in amulets by the devout.

Some buildings are also constructed as *mandalas*, the most notable being Borobudur at Java and the Potala Palace at Lhasa.

The serenity of Khechopalri Lake, a short walk away from the *gompa* of the same name, is said to derive from its sacred nature

Khechopalri

Literally, the Noble Heaven-Reaching Mountain. The monastery is situated half an hour's walk from the sacred Khechopalri Lake, a lake so calm it is said to be protected from all disturbances. Locals insist that not even a leaf falls on it to disturb its placidity; and if one does, a bird immediately swoops down to carry it off. Khechopalri Lake is the venue of a major tourist festival in March.

Sangacholing

Situated on a ridge above Pelling and the famous *gompa* at Pemayangtse, it can be reached only after a 40-minute trek up a steep, forested hill. Sangacholing, literally Place of Secret Spells, is among the oldest monasteries in the state, having been built in 1697.

Dubdi

It is the oldest monastery in Sikkim and was consecrated after the coronation of the first Chogyal in 1642. It is located above Yuksam, the place where the first coronation took place, among verdant forests and can be reached only after an arduous trek.

Dubdi, the oldest monastery in Sikkim

Butter Sculpture

A work of art peculiar to Tibetan Buddhism is sculpting images from butter. The annual Monlam Chenmo festival at Enchey monastery is a good time and place to get a glimpse of this art.

Yak butter is highly-valued and is extensively used in rituals. Easily malleable, it is moulded into images of many sizes – from small but intricate tutelary deities to great life-size statues.

Unlike other forms of Buddhist ritual art, there are no canons dictating the creation of butter sculptures and so there is great spontaniety on show. Popular motifs include animals, especially dragons, and the Mahakala demon-god.

Prayer

As in most other religions, prayer beads are an indispensable ritual implement of Buddhism as well. The beads, usually 108 of them, are used to count *mantras*. The most popular are beads made of sandalwood or of the seeds of the Bodhi tree, while beads carved out of human bones or *raksha* seeds in a string of 60 are used for more arcane ritual-chants.

Phensog

This Nyingmapa monastery was built in 1721 by Lama Jigme Pawo, said to be the third incarnation of the famous Lhatsun Chempo. It was destroyed in a fire in 1947 but was restored soon after.

In fact, the *gompa* today has been renovated yet again and makes for a worthy stopover on a trip to North Sikkim from Gangtok. Most tourists tend to miss out Phensog as the tour operators are more keen to take them on to the more frequented Phodong monastery further ahead. Insist on stopping here to take in the solace bred by remoteness. Phensog's annual *chaam* dance is held two days before Loosong.

Right:
A painting of
Guru Rimpoche from
Phensog monastery

A *thanka* hanging in Phodong monastery
Below:
The annual *chaam* at Phodong
Opposite Page:
Monasteries come vibrantly alive at festivals like the Phang Labsol being celebrated here

Phodong

The Royal Chapel, some 40 kms from Gangtok on North Sikkim highway is a bustling monastery of the Kagyu sect. Located on a hilltop, it was built by Chogyal Gyurmed Namgyal in the beginning of the 18th century. Phodong monastery's main festival falls on the 28th and 29th day of the tenth month of the Tibetan calendar when *chaam* dances are ritually performed.

The annual *chaam* dance of Lachung monastery
Overleaf: Monks tread the measure in the Lachung *chaam*

Lachung

Built around 1880, this *gompa* of the Nyingma sect is among the quietest in Sikkim. Situated amid apple orchards across the river from the town-centre, it is framed against a range of snow-topped mountains. Visitors will usually find its wicker gate locked, but jump over it to reach one of the architecturally most distinctive monasteries in Sikkim. Notable especially are the dragons over the porch and the paintings on either flank.

Apart from these main *gompas*, Sikkim is studded with several smaller monasteries.

Bermoik

This Nyingma monastery built in 1952 is situated just above Singtam in South Sikkim.

Gnathang

The only Gelugpa monastery in Sikkim, it is situated near the Tibetan border.

Kwezing
Located near the town of the same name, this monastery was built in the last decade of the 19th century during the reign of Thutob Namgyal.

Lingtem
This monastery is located within the Lepcha reserve of Dzongu in North Sikkim.

Namchi
Located in the headquarter town of the South district, this monastery was built during the early half of the 18th century.

Ralong
Situated near Ravangla in South Sikkim, this is the oldest Kagyupa monastery in Sikkim.

Shurishing Yungdrung Dungdrakling
The only monastery of the Bon religion, it is located near Sosing in South Sikkim.

Simik
Situated near Singtam town in East Sikkim, this monastery was built during the reign of Chogyal Tsudphud Namgyal at the tail-end of the 18th century.

Sinon
With a name that literally means Suppressor of Fear, this early 18th century monastery is located some 10 kms above Tashiding.

Yangang
Literally the Ridge of Fortune, this monastery built in 1840 is located in Yangang village, some 10 kms downhill from Ravangla in South Sikkim.

Zurmang Kagyud
Perhaps Sikkim's youngest monastery, it was set up in 1999 and is located on a fork off the main road to Rumtek, some 25 kms out of Gangtok.

Hidden Treasure
The Nyingmapa Buddhists believe that Guru Rimpoche hid many collections of sacred literature in secret locations. A whole class of diviners called *tertons* or treasure hunters has historically spent lifetimes searching for these valuable treasures.

Literature

The great monasteries dotting the highlands, from Ladakh in the extreme west through Sikkim, Bhutan and Tibet, have impressive libraries, filled with a vast corpus of religious literature. The books are mostly in Tibetan, which has, over the centuries, acquired somewhat the status of Latin, in that it is the language of classical literature. In Sikkim, we find in addition to this great Tibetan treasury, a remarkable collection of writing in the Lepcha language.

The books that line shelves in Sikkimese monasteries are reverentially draped in silk and placed between wooden boards for protection. This is one of the images of Pemayangtse that struck western travellers in the 18th century and also remains the image the modern tourist takes away today. Strictly speaking, these are not books but prints on bark, painstakingly made from wooden xylographs.

Today the Dharmachakra Centre at Rumtek houses the largest collection of monastic literature. And a visit to the monastery will show the *lotsbas* or lama-translators diligently rendering the great literature of Sanskrit and Chinese into Tibetan. The Namgyal Research Institute of Tibetology in Gangtok also houses a well-preserved literature collection.

The main body of Tibetan Buddhist literature comprises the *Kangyur* and the *Tengyur*. These primary texts are found in all monasteries. The *Kangyur* contains faithful translations of *Tripitaka* or the *Three Baskets*, the earliest canonical Buddhist literature in Pali. The Tangyur is an enormous collection of commentaries on the *Kangyur* books.

By far the most popular books today are those of proverbs, which every young monk in Sikkim learns by rote. The *Songs of Milarepa*, the national poet of Tibet, is ever inspiring and sung even today by many lamas.

Another book contains hymns in praise of the mighty Khang-chen-dzonga, the mountain god of Sikkim. Composed by the venerable Lhatsun Chempo, it is the standard manual for worshipping the great mountain god.

Then, there are the *Debther* and the *Namthar*, the histories of the *gompas* and the great lamas respectively. These treatises have been written by famous monk-historians like Bu-ton Rimpoche and Padma Karpo.

During the 18th century, a Lepcha script was devised, which then became the medium in which a number of great books were written, including *Tashi Sun* a fabulous history of Padmasambava, and *Ek Doshi Mantom*, a manual for rituals.

Another celebrated secular work of Sikkim is the *Tales of Gesarling*. Its inspiring stories tell of a hero who comes with his army from the mythical land of Shambala in times of crisis to vanquish evil.

Below:
The sacred books, wrapped in silk and carefully housed in the library at Rumtek
Opposite Page:
The holy books being carried in procession around the streets of Gangtok on the occasion of Saga Dawa, the most important of Buddhist festivals

EAST SIKKIM

East Sikkim is the entry point for all travellers heading for Gangtok and North Sikkim from Bagdogra or Siliguri. One enters the mountain state at Rangpo where permits are scrutinised. From Rangpo, the 40-km drive up to the capital Gangtok keeps pace with the Teesta and is a pleasure beyond compare. Stop by wherever you can and walk down to the river for a paddle in its icy waters. Just before Melli, also watch out for the spot where the greener waters of the Rangeet swell into the Teesta.

Below:
An artist's impression of Gangtok
Previous Page:
The confluence of the Teesta and the Rangeet

Gangtok

Gangtok, literally High Hill, is located on a ridge overlooking the Ranipool river. An altitude of 1,870 metres ensures that this city is wreathed in clouds for a large part of the year. Gangtok is a remarkable for its location: Set among lush paddy terraces and river-watered valleys it commands a stunning view of the higher Himalayan ranges.

Unlike most other hill stations of India, Gangtok has an amazing sense of civic values. Street litter is almost unknown and even the smallest shop has a dustbin beside its doors; traffic and parking regulations are followed almost religiously; and the people of Gangtok are refreshingly polite and unfailingly cheerful.

Map courtesy: Sikkim Tourism

Timing
9 am-12.30 pm
1.30 pm-3.30 pm
(closed Sunday and every second Saturday of the month)
Phone: 23126/22928

Directorate of Handicrafts and Handlooms

A kilometre uphill from the main market is the state-run emporium of handicrafts. An array of local handicrafts, including *thankas, choktses* or lacquered tables, carpets, masks, handmade paper, is available on sale here.

Timing
10 am-4 pm on weekdays
10 am-2 pm on holidays and Sundays
Entry fee: Rs 2
Phone: 81525

Namgyal Research Institute of Tibetology

About a kilometre downhill from the main market on MG Road stands the country's finest data source on Tibetology. The Institute, itself a fine example of Tibetan Buddhist architecture, is a repository of relics and books on the Tibetan culture.

It houses some 30,000 documents, mostly xylographs (printed using wooden slabs embossed with text in reverse), as well as rare bark manuscripts. The Institute also holds an invaluable collection of antiques like statues, *thankas*, and coins.

Do-Drul Chorten

Also called Phurba, this *chorten* is located on a hillock adjacent to the Tibetology Institute. The towering *chorten* is surrounded by 108 prayer wheels inscribed with the holy *mantra, Om Mani Padme Hum*. It was built in the late 1940s under the auspices of Trulsi Rimpoche, the then head of the Nyingma order. At the head of the road leading to the *chorten* is a rock called the To Da Bu or Stone Horse, that lends its name to the area as well.

Ganesh Tok

Situated on the Ridge, 7 kms from Gangtok, is a temple to Lord Ganesh so small that it allows only one person in at a time and even that person has to crawl to get in. The shrine has a bird's eye view of the sprawling town from 2,031 metres, while across the hills are the peaks of the Khang-chen-dzonga and Siniolchu.

Hanuman Tok

11 kms away from Gangtok, perched above Ganesh Tok, is a functioning shrine dedicated

to Hanuman. The temple has a panoramic view and a short distance before the staircase leading to the temple is the burial ground of the royal family. A series of *stupas* and *chortens* mark the royal graves.

Timing
8 am-11am
8 am-5 pm on holidays
Phone: 23126/22928

Himalayan Zoological Park

Centred across the road from Ganesh Tok, this 205-hectare park is known locally as Bulbuley and houses various animals including the rare red panda.

Saramsa Garden

Fourteen kms away from Gangtok lies this orchid garden with rare flowers and exotic plants of the tropical and temperate type.

White Hall

This building on the Ridge is named for J Claude White the first British political officer in Sikkim. It is, today, a club with all the fine appendages of one.

Timing
9 am–12.30 pm
1.30 pm–3.30 pm
(closed Sunday)
Entry fee: Rs 5

Flower Exhibition Centre

Close to the White Hall is the place where flower shows are held round the year. The special attraction is the orchid show during the spring tourist season.

Tsukhlakhang Monastery

Located in the Palace Complex near the Ridge is this two-storeyed chapel used for ceremonial occasions in the royal family, like births, weddings and coronations.

Enchey Monastery

The monastery known literally as the High, Strong Place is located next to the Tourist Lodge in Gangtok. It was originally a small hermitage and only became a proper monastery in 1909. It belongs to the Nyingma sect and its main festival is held in January.

The path up from the car park is always strung over with prayer flags and the row of prayer wheels lining the way are constantly aspin as those coming to the *gompa* make this traditional gesture of devotion.

Above:
Lall Bazaar with its stalls selling fresh vegetables, heady spices, glass beads and bangles is one of the most picturesque sights of Gangtok

Excursions

Kabi Longstok

The place where blood brotherhood pact between the Lepchas and the Bhutias was signed is 17 kms along the North Sikkim highway. There is a memorial pillar marking the historic spot.

Rumtek Monastery

24 kms away from Gangtok is the Rumtek Dharmachakra Centre, the seat of the Kagyu sect, which houses some unique religious objects. (*see page* 74-75)

Zurmang Kagyud Monastery

Sikkim's newest monastery is located at Lingdum, close to the Rumtek *gompa*. It is worth visiting for its exquisite architecture.

Kyongnosla Alpine Sanctuary

Some 31 kms from Gangtok starts this sanctuary that harbours rare animals like the red panda, the Himalayan marmot and the Tibetan fox. Sights within the wildlife park include the Tseten Tashi cave.

Tumlong

Ruins of the place that served as capital of Sikkim for the large part of the 19th century.

Fambong La Wildlife Sanctuary

Located some 25 kms away from Gangtok is this wildlife park with an area of 51.76 sq kms. Oak and bamboo, rhododendrons and orchids and a wide range of animals and birds make this biodiversity reserve the ideal trekkers' destination.

Log Huts within the Reserve are available at Golaytar and Tumin at Rs 50 per person per night.
Entry fee: Rs 5
For permission: Chief Wildlife Warden, Forest Secretariat, Deorali, Gangtok
Phone: 80191

Tsomgo Lake

This oval-shaped lake is situated some 40 kms away from Gangtok on the old trade route to Tibet. Usually placid through the year, the lake, at an altitude of 3,700 metres, freezes over completely in winter. There is a small Shiva temple by the lake and the area around it is a riot of colour in spring when the primulas and rhododendrons bloom. A km long and some 15 metres deep, it plays host to many migratory birds including the Brahminy Duck, when the winter gives over. The drive to Tsomgo is quite spectacular, with numerous waterfalls and mountain torrents breaking the breath-taking green.

Sikkimese folklore tells of how the Tsomgo Lake came to be where it is. According to popular belief, the lake was originally situated a distance away. One night, an old woman who lived at Tsomgo dreamt that the Lake was about to move there. She warned her two yak-herder friends of the impending move but when they didn't take her seriously, made preparations to leave by herself. She milked her dri or the female yak, poured a little of the milk on the ground in a traditionally auspicious gesture, and left.

As she was leaving, she saw an inordinately fair lady, with gleaming white hair, carding yarn as she walked. As soon as she appeared the earth turned into water and thus was the Tsomgo born. Needless to say, the two doubting yak-herders drowned in the waters, along with their herds.

All tourists headed for Tsomgo need a special permit. While Indian travellers can pick up this permit in Gangtok from the Superintendent of Police, Checkpost Division, foreigners need to apply to the tourism department and can only travel in groups of at least two persons. They are best advised to go through a travel agent recognised by the government of Sikkim. Also, private vehicles and buses are not allowed here; one has to travel by government approved taxis organised through a travel agent.

SOUTH SIKKIM

Namchi, literally Sky High, is the capital of the South Sikkim district, which is composed largely of paddy terraces so green that they are an instant eye-toner. At 1,660 metres, **Namchi** looks across a vast valley at the mountains.

High above Namchi is a flat stretch of land at 2,580 metres surrounded by deep forests. This is Tendong Hill, a traditional retreat for lamas who use the solitude of its height as an ideal place to meditate. Reached after a two-hour trek from **Damthang**, 13 kms away from Namchi and the nearest roadhead, it still retains an air of reflection about it.

Above:
The Nepali ceremony of *tika* on the occasion of Dasain, the most important festival in the Nepali calendar
Facing page:
Smiling Nepali faces are the most visible part of South Sikkim's population

Hotels and Lodges in South Sikkim

Hotels/Lodges	Phone
Melli	
10 Zing	60506
Holiday Melli	70224
Mainam View	60610
Mainamla	60666
Manokamana	60862
Mt Narsing	60717
Pradhan	70243
South Point	60851
Swallow's Nest	60847
Namthang	
Jinlob	
Krishna	
Mount View	41221
Tendong	41215

Lepcha legend also says that **Tendong**, literally Upraised Horn, was the place that saved their tribe from an ancient flood. In a story that has parallels with that of Noah's Ark, the Lepchas tell of a time when the gods sent down a great flood to wipe out the world and its ills. Tendong rose 'like a great horn' above the waters and provided the Lepchas a safe place to retreat to.

Another 20 kms from Damthang lies **Ravangla**, a popular transit point with trekkers. It has several short nature trails and treks to **Menam Hill** and **Borong** to offer, as well as a trip to **Sharchok Pephu**, one of the four sacred caves of Sikkim, 5 kms away. Also check out the monastery at **Kewzing**, 10 kms away, which is the only one owing affiliation to the Bon religion.

Ravangla is situated at the base of Menam Hill, whose 3,116 metres-height affords one of the most glorious views in Sikkim. The Khang-chen-dzonga range, of course, looms ahead in full glory, but on a clear day, the sharp-eyed can even look out at the plains of north Bengal on the other side.

Take a walk to **Bhaley Dunga**, the rocky spur that juts out from the hill directly above **Yangang** village.

To reach the village one has to walk in famous footsteps – the tortuous hill-path down to Yangang is one of the recorded routes taken by the famous 19th century botanist, Sir Joseph D Hooker. The other popular trek route here is the four-hour walk to Borong, a picturesque little village with a hot-spring.

The government-run **Temi Tea Garden** is Sikkim's only tea estate. It rolls down the slopes below Tendong Hill and a drive through it is one of the loveliest experiences in Sikkim. The road up to the factory, where one can watch the tea leaves being processed, is marked by delicate cherry trees. Temi tea is available easily in Gangtok, and is suffused with the fragrance of these hills.

Jorethang
Janta
Jigmee
Kasturi
Namgyal
Rangit Valley
Zongri

Kewzing
Fampho
Penkeyla

Namchi
Chang
Dokham
Keshang
Mayal
Nayuma
Note:
- STD code for South Sikkim is 03595.
- List of Hotels provided by Sikkim Tourism

WEST SIKKIM

For mountaineers and trekkers as well as for nature-seeking tourists, West Sikkim is perhaps the most frequented of Sikkim's regions. The famous Dzongri trail and the magnificent Pemayangtse *gompa* are both in the district of West Sikkim. The region is beautiful, with fast-paced streams threading their turbulent way through deep green forests.

The district headquarters of West Sikkim is at **Gyaltshing**, a little town arranged around a square, which springs to colourful life every Monday with a weekly *haat*.

Below:
Nepali women at Gyaltshing's weekly *haat*
Right:
Khang-chen-dzonga as seen from Pelling
Facing Page:
A fish-eye view of the main entrance to Pemayangtse monastery

A few kilometres away from Gyaltshing are the magnificent ruins of **Rabdantse**, the 17th century capital of the early Chogyals, which was abandoned towards the end of the 18th century when it came under threat from Nepal. Walk or drive through the woods to reach the remains of the Palace; the chortens around the site have, remarkably, withstood the ravages of time. The Archaeological Survey of India is engaged in excavations at the site.

Some 10 kms away from Gyaltshing lies **Pelling**, which is fast becoming a crowded urban settlement. Situated at an altitude of 2,058 metres, its stunning view of the entire Khang-chen-dzonga range has begun to draw tourists in hordes. As a result several tourist lodges and hotels have mushroomed all across the town, making it rather crammed.

Close by are two 17th century monasteries of Sikkim – the famous **Pemayangtse** and the more remote **Sangacholing**. Visit them for their distinctive architecture and the view they offer of religion as a way of life.

Yaks

This doughty animal is indispensable to life in Sikkim. It is a beast of burden and also a provider of milk, meat, and wool; even its droppings are used as fuel. Yak milk is made into *churpi*, the local cheese that forms the main ingredient in a number of Sikkimese dishes, while yak butter laces the local brew of tea.

Yaks are remarkably sure-footed and can carry upto 60 kg-70 kg of weight up steep slopes for hours at a stretch. Not only do yaks forage on their own, but they also require no grooming or stabling, making them a low-maintenance domestic animal. The yak crossbred with the cow gives the dzo, which can survive at lower altitudes.

Strangely enough, in North Sikkim where they are the most numerous, Yaks are not brought down from the high altitudes for the winter. As the wind blows hard and sharp on the higher slopes, it clears away the snow and frost from the ground, thus exposing grass on which the animals can graze. Yak-herders' huts have also proved invaluable to weary trekkers in the less touristy trekking trails.

The annual yak race in Muguthang in North Sikkim during the festival of Drukpa Teshi is a popular event in Sikkim's local calendar. The state government also runs Yak safaris to Dzongri.

Hotels and Lodges in West Sikkim

Hotels/Lodges	Phone
Gyaltshing	
Mayalu	
Anchal	50869
Attri	50602
Kanchanzanga	50789
Dentam	
Devika	55269
Lerena	
Pravesh	55503
Singshore	55235
Suriya	55238
Legship	
Trishna	50887
Pelling	
Bintam	50682
Chinari	58256
Garuda	50614
Heaven	58238
Hindusthan Lodge	58247
Kabur	58504
Kailash	58257
Kecheperi	50681
Mondal Lodge	50684
Namgay	58269
Norbu Gang	50566
Panchok	58237
Panorama	58274
Parazong	58239
Pemachen	50641
Phamrong	50660
Pradhan	50615
Resort Stellate	50571
Samtenling	58335
Sangha	58322
Sarita	50624
Sikkim Tourist Centre	50855
Silver Park	58253
Simboo	58246
Sinchur	58288
Sister Guest House	50569
Sitara	58211
Snow White	58246
Sonam Delek	58286
Sun	58207
Tashiling	58287
Touristo	58206
View Point	58280
Window Park	58212

Above:
Day-break
at Yuksam
Right:
A luminously
green trekking
trail above Yuksam

Other places to see include the **Singshore Bridge** at Uttarey, one of Sikkim's landmarks in that it is the highest bridge in the mountain state.

Drive up via Sombaria to the little mountain village of **Hilley** at 2,972 metres, which is the launch-point for a trek through the **Versay Rhododendron Sanctuary**. Versay itself, at an altitude of 3,056 metres, has an interesting place to stay – the Shambhala Mountain Resort.

Pemayangtse

Mt Pandim	50756

Soreng

Deep
Hill Top
Ladenla
Lotus
Mid Way
Pemathang
Rodhi
Uma
Yanki

Tashiding

Blue Bird	43248
Siniolchu	43211

Tikjuk

Kyi De Khang	50964
Zongri	50644

Uttarey

Green Valley	55258
Singa Lilla	55261

Yangtey

Tashi Gang	50340

Yuksam

Arpon
Demazong
Dzongrilla
Pemathang
TashiGang
Wild Orchid
Yongri Gang

Bikshthang

The Bliss Resort	52284

Note:
- STD code for West Sikkim is 03595.
- List of Hotels provided by Sikkim Tourism

NORTH SIKKIM

Nowhere does the amazing biodiversity of Sikkim come through so strongly as it does in North Sikkim. From the lush tropicality of the area around Mangan, the district headquarter, through the rhododendron forests beyond Lachung to unexplored and uncompromising wilderness of the heights that merge into the Tibetan Plateau -this district of Sikkim is an ever-changing panorama.

It is sparsely populated and unspoilt, and the government and people are keen to keep it that way. All tourists, domestic or foreign, need a special permit to travel here and the entry of private cars is blocked at Chungthang sub-division. North Sikkim can be toured only through tour operators recognised by the state government.

Hotels and Lodges in North Sikkim

Hotels/Lodges	Phone
Mangan	
Lachen Valley	
Himalayan	
Mt. View	
KJ Lachenpa	34472
Chuchey	34503
Ganga	34506
Didi	34732
Kalden	34504
Lachen Valley	34333
	34444
North Point	34505
View Lodge	34747
Muslim	
Karma	
Phodong	
NewNorthway	62953
Jyoti	62903
Northway	60771
Yak & Yeti	60884
Namok	
Choley	60506
Lachung	
Le Coxy	
Resort	25113
	23330
Lalligurash	27185
Guest House	25113
Apple Resort	
Alpine Resort	
Dabia Inn	
River View	
Lodge	
Pine View	
Kalden Lodge	
Gyatso Lodge	
Orchid Lodge	60747
Wild Orchid	
Lodge	60610
Primula Lodge	60666
Yumthang	
Valley Inn	60862
Snow Lion	
Inn Resort	60717
Strawberry Inn	60845
Sonam Inn	60623
Kalden Lodge	60638
Dallas Inn	60851
Seyla Inn	60847
Blue Sky	
Lodge	25113

Although it is fast-becoming popular among travellers looking for a break from the beaten path, North Sikkim is quite innocent of tourist paraphernalia or facilities. Accommodation, when available, is primitive and travelling here is an adventure sport in itself.

It is best to opt for a four-wheel drive when heading north because the highway is most prone to the caprices of nature. 'You are approaching a SINKING AREA' – this alarming sign, looms ahead at regular intervals, signalling stretches where the shifting soil of the young Himalayas has turned the land pulpy. Incidentally, this road north is the region's lifeline. All aids and amenities to living, from telephones to electricity to fuel supply, flow along it and when the road closes, so do all.

The drive from Gangtok to North Sikkim initially goes gently downhill through tropical vegetation dominated by banana plantations. The road is broken by ribbons of rivers that wash across it. Rongrongchu, Langthechu, Richu – the mountain streams are many and magnificent. Bridges are built but often washed away; but their going occasions little surprise and even less dismay among the locals.

Left:
Gurgling mountain streams are almost constant companions on the journey through North Sikkim.
Previous page:
The Yumthang valley peppered with snow
Below:
The Chungthang valley

Mangan is a small, sleepy town that overlooks the Teesta. Across the river lies the Lepcha reserve of Dzongu. The road from Mangan to Chungthang, shadows the Teesta, going through dense forests. Those without a Protected Area Permit are stopped at Toong Bridge, 12 kms short of Chungthang,

Chungthang is a little town in a lush basin ringed with high mountains. Nestled deep as it is, its horizon is high and limited and the sun rises later and sets earlier here than places just outside this tiny valley.

The town itself is at an altitude of 1,750 metres and marks the confluence of the snow-waters of the Lachen and Lachung rivers. The valley in which the town is located is rich in natural life. Arrive in the spring and you'll find the town lined with lillies, planted and cared for by the soldiers of the Indian Army stationed there.

The high spot in Chungthang is the rock believed to bear Guru Padmasambhava's footprint. The area around bears lush paddy despite high altitude aridity. It is said that Guru Padmasambhava once scattered some rice grains here and the area has continued to produce paddy since then.

Above:
Lachen village with the monastery on the hill above it.
Facing Page:
Paddy fields in Lachung valley

Just out of Chungthang, take the road that wheels right and head for the Bhutia township of **Lachen**, 28 kms away. Surrounded by apple orchards and open scrubland inlaid with bunches of wildflower, Lachen is alluring in its simplicity. A short distance before the township is the Lachen monastery, more than a century-and-a-half old.

Its echo lies across to the east, in **Lachung**, a spreading Bhutia village that sprawls across the two banks of the Lachung river. The focal point of local life is the monastery across the highway.

The Lachen and Lachung valleys run northward to the stupendous mass of the Himalayan range which divides Sikkim from Tibet. The two narrow vales have high flanks and are separated by a range extending southward, which rises from a base-elevation of 3,000 metres.

The journey from Chungthang to Lachung is a soul-refreshing experience – the drive is just about 22 kms long, and almost each twist of the road brings to sight a mountain torrent cascading down the hill-slope, each sparkling waterfall glistening against the deep green of the forest.

Lachung village offers basic accommodation, but it is the only place to stay on the road to Yumthang. Food all along this highway is only noodles and *thukpa* and, of course, *chhang*.

Landslides

Rapid deforestation as well as unchecked mining and quarrying have resulted in the fast denudation of Sikkim's hill slopes. The soil erosion has meant that landslides are a common and constant hazard, especially so in North Sikkim.

Landslides occur so often that the locals have devised a way of dealing with them, as well as a nomenclature around the occurrence. 'Trans-shipment' is the ingenious method of crossing a landslide blocking the road by climbing the mountain and hopping across the landslide at its very head. Porters and guides appear as though from nowhere at the site of a road-block, offering to ferry bag and baggage across.

The high point of any trip north out of Gangtok is the journey between Lachung and Yumthang, where the road climbs more than 1,000 metres in less than 25 kms. This road runs through the **Singba Rhododendron Reserve**, and is awash with colour in spring when the rhododendrons are in bloom. Some 46 varieties of rhododendrons can be found here, amid forests of juniper, spruce and hemlock.

Lachen
Guru Dongmar Lodge
Snow Peak Lodge 41221
Toga Lodge 41215
Juniper Resort 28577

Thangu
Tseten Tashi Lodge

Rangrang
Subedar Hotel

Chungthang
Kyipsong
Sonam Hotel
Pema Ghasal Hotel
Neelam Hotel

Singhik
SinghikTourist Lodge

Note:
- STD code for North Sikkim is 03592.
- List of Hotels provided by Sikkim Tourism

Rhododendrons

Sir J D Hooker, the famous botanist who travelled through Sikkim in 1850, writes: 'The banks of rivers between 2,500 metres and 4,000 metres are generally covered with rhododendrons, sometimes to the near exclusion of other wooded vegetation, especially near the snowy mountains – a cool temperature and great humidity, being the most favourable conditions for the luxurious growth of this species'.

Rhododendrons may truly be called the glory of Sikkim, so beautiful are they and also so abundant in this mountain land. A trek through the Singalila or Chola ranges or a drive to the Yumthang valley, takes one through miles of rhododendron trees ablaze with flowers in shades ranging from white, through yellow, pink and red.

There are some 40 species to be seen on the slopes of Sikkim's mountains, varying in size from the gigantic *R. grande*, a tree of some 9-12 metres and trunk that girdles 1.5 metres, to the almost prostrate *R. nivale*, barely raising its head

two inches above the ground. A few species are found as low as 1,800 metres, but the majority grows between 2,700 metres and 4,200 metres. Four species (*R. lepidotum, nivale, setosum* and *anthopagon*) can also be seen above 4,500 metres.

At about 1,800 metres, *Dalhousie* with its large flowers, is usually the first to appear. It is a small straggly epiphytic shrub, usually found clinging to the tops of trees.

The *falconerii* is a large gregarious shrub, with large leathery leaves felted on the underside with rust-coloured hairs. It can be found above 2,700 metres. The widely distributed *arboreum* can be commonly seen up to

3,000 metres.

Only one species, *R. cinnabarinum*, is said to be poisonous. Hooker mentions this, saying, '...many of the young goats and kids died after eating it, foaming at the mouth and grinding their teeth'. He also notes that the much sought-after honey of the wild bee is eschewed by locals during spring for that is when it is said to be poisoned by rhododendron flowers.

Rhododendrons are devoid of strong perfume, with the exception of *R anthopagon*, *setosum* and *nivale*. These three, when crushed underfoot or otherwise bruised, exude an overpowering scent. The twigs of these plants are burned in monasteries as incense.

Some 135 kms from Gangtok, **Yumthang** town is a nondescript village inhabited for the most part by nomadic yak herders. It is popular for its hot springs, located to the left beyond a bridge over the Lachung river. A bathing hut has been constructed over two pools of the sulphur-infused water, immensely popular among the locals for their natural curative powers.

A Forest Department Log Hut with two rooms available is the only place to stay in Yumthang but getting permission to do so is not easy.

The treeline in Sikkim goes up to some 4,500 metres, so Yumthang at 3,564 metres is quite well-treed. Take a short drive to the Shiv Mandir – peopled by five soldiers and 12 dogs – above Yumthang and drink in the delights of an alpine forest, with its graceful trees of silver fir and larch, with the Donkia peak looming above.

Above:
The glacial waters of the Tso Lhamu lake
Left:
Primulas on the way to Yumthang

Further north of the Lachen-Lachung valleys are the lands few visit – Thangu, the Lhonak Valley, Muguthang, Donkiala, and the jewel lakes of Gurudongmar and Tso Lhamu. Falling in the rainshadow of the mighty Himalayas, the landscape of this part of Sikkim is harsh and bleak, and only the hardy yak-herders call it home.

ADVENTURE TRAILS

Sikkim is the destination incomparable for those looking for a dose of adventure. From trekking to mountaineering through river running and mountain biking, it offers a range of activities to those seeking thrill therapy.

Mountain Biking

Of late Sikkim has also started offering mountain biking as an adventure activity. Apart from the sheer charge of the sport there are Sikkim's spectacular views on offer.

Mountain bikes can be hired from registered tour operators at economical rates. The most popular stretches are centred on Gangtok and include the road between Sajong and Ramka and from MG Road and Tashi View Point.

River Rafting

The white waters of the Teesta and the Rangeet offer some good stretches of thrilling rapids. Sikkim Toursim organises some trips in the frothing lower reaches of both. Some private travel agents in Gangtok also offer these rides.

Makha – Rangpo

This is a beginner's stretch and offers some spectacular scenery on the banks as you rush past Sirwani and Mamring.

Sikip – Melli

This roller-coaster ride down the Rangeet goes past Jorethang and Majitar.

Bordang – Melli

Head to Bordang for a swirling ride down the Teesta. The rapids vary from grades 2, 3, and 4 during the four-and-a-half hour ride.

Kayaking

The stout-hearted can take a thrilling ride down Sikkim's many rivers in fibreglass kayaks.

Rafting & Kayaking
Contact the Sikkim Tourism Office on M G Road in Gangtok. **Phone:** 22634 **Fax:** 20352

Trekking season
March-May;
Sept-Nov
However, trekking to altitudes above 4,250 metres should be avoided till April, because snow continues to lie on the ground and some places can even experience fresh snow fall.

Trekking

Sikkim is a trekker's paradise – all areas have beauty to recommend them: The near-tropical lushness of South Sikkim, the snow mountains of East Sikkim, the awesome wilderness of North Sikkim. However, most of the more popular trekking routes are the ones in West Sikkim.

For those interested in going trekking in the interiors of Sikkim, the department of tourism issues a Protected Area Permit (PAP) at Gangtok, which is available for a specified area for groups consisting of two or more, provided the trekking programme is arranged through a registered travel agency.

You do not require experience to go trekking but you must be physically fit. It is necessary to begin exercising weeks before you start a trek. Before starting, plan out your route and arrange for maps and necessary permits. Choose your trekking route on the basis of time available to you, and the season.

Trekkers' huts are available along the more well-trod routes in West Sikkim. The facilities in these are very basic, but if you chart a careful route you can do without carrying tents along. Run by the Sikkim government, they usually comprise a couple of rooms provided with basic linen and the caretaker can generally rustle up a meal, especially if you have booked in advance.

Below:
The forest rest house at Yumthang which is used by trekkers

Trekking Essentials

- Tent
- Sleeping bag
- Boots (preferably ones with thermo-plastic rubber or TPR soles; also must be well worn to prevent untimely blisters)
- Woollen socks (multiple pairs)
- Cotton socks (to wear under the woollen ones)
- UV protector goggles
- Rope
- Spare shoelaces
- Batteries (spares too)
- Cotton inners
- Head torch
- Sunhat
- Water bottle
- Umbrella (doubles up as walking stick)
- String
- Safety pins
- Plastic bags
- Note pad
- Pen
- Candles
- Matchbox
- Gas cylinders and stove
- Rations (including fresh juices, glucose and chocolates)
- Woollens (warm jackets, sweaters)

Trekking Tips

It is advisable to arrange your trekking equipment before you come to India, although most of it is available here.

There are many trekking agencies that provide equipment on hire. A good agency should provide camp equipment, see to the food rations and also the cooking, plan the trekking stages, liase with locals and make decisions regarding progress.

While making bookings, make sure that the agency will provide a leader who is qualified and familiar with the route. Keep all your travel documents and permits at hand, as they have to be produced at different points for checking by the police and other security agencies. Keep the papers in a plastic cover to prevent them from getting wet.

Leave your valuables in the hotel locker and keep your cameras and other expensive equipment safely as these can be easy targets for thieves.

You must not trek alone as it is difficult to arrange for help if you get injured or fall sick.

Do not drink water from streams and rivers even if it appears to be pure. Carry your own supply of water and high-energy food items like chocolates, nuts and chips as local food may upset your digestive system.

Walk at a comfortable pace. Do not try to cover too much. Rest as much as you feel like. Take frequent breaks to enjoy the views. Take plenty of fluids to prevent dehydration and shield your face from the sun which can be particularly harsh at these altitudes..

Leeches
Watch out for these blood-sucking creepies at all times and on all routes. The only way to get rid of one if it clings to you is to either pour salt on it or to burn it off with a lit cigarette.

Below:
Trekkers on the Dzongri trail

Yuksam-Dzongri Trek

(Season: April-mid June; September-November)

One of the most trodden of trails in Sikkim because it is one of the few routes open to foreigners.

Yuksam (1,676 metres) can be attained by road (via Gyaltshing) from Gangtok. It has several trekkers' huts as well as a hotels and guides; porters and yaks are all easily available, as is trekking equipment like tents and sleeping bags. The porters charge around Rs 100 per day, while yaks can be hired for Rs 150 per day.

This was the place where the first Chogyal was crowned in 1642 and the wooden altar and stone throne can be seen in a peaceful pine forest above the Kathok Lake.

Day 1: Yuksam to Tsokha

It takes about 9 hours to traverse the 16 kms between Yuksam and Tsokha. The first hour is across relatively flat land, criss-crossed by small gurgling streams, a leap wide. A four-hour climb, scrunching underfoot the leaves that fall from trees lining the path takes one to Bakhim.

Bakhim (2,740 metres), which has a Forest Bungalow by way of accommodation. Tsokha (2,950 metres) is a further three hours' away, and has a trekkers' hut and a private lodge, as well as a camping site, for overnight stay.

Day 2: Tsokha to Dzongri

A morning's trek through massed rhododendron trees takes one to Dzongri via Phedang with its magnificent view of snow peaks like Pandim, Narsingh and of course, the mighty Khang-chen-dzonga. Another hour uphill and one reaches the ridge from where the descent to Dzongri (4,030 metres and 10 kms from Bakhim) begins. There is a camping ground as well as two trekkers' huts here. An hour-and-a-half's walk from the huts takes one to Dzongrila, the pass from where the entire Khang-chen-dzonga range is visible.

At Dzongri the bridle path forks, the left leads to the Base Camp of the Himalayan Mountaineering Institute (4,573 metres and 9 kms away) and the other heads towards Gochala.

Day 3: Dzongri to Thangshing

The trail climbs the ridge through rhododendron and juniper trees until the crest some 5 kms away and then descends across the Prek river. A gentle climb along the river takes one to Thangshing (3,900 metres) and its trekkers' hut and camping ground.

Day 4: Thangshing to Sunghmoten Lake

A trek through scrubland and, later, a moraine takes one to the point where the trail drops away to the glacial waters of the Sunghmoten Lake. The views of the Khang-chen-dzonga range in this section are stunning. The Lake (4250 metres) has a trekkers' hut. Gochala (4900metres) is attained after a brief halt at Zemathang (4800 metres). The whole trail, incidentally through moraine, moves literally in the shadow of the overwhelming Khang-chen-dzonga. Return to Sunghmoten Lake.

Day 7: Sunghmoten Lake to Tsokha

Return by a lower route from Thangshing along the Prek river, avoiding Dzongri altogether.

Monastery Trek

(Season: March-May, September-December)

Day 1: Pelling to Pemayangtse

Make Pelling the base for this trek as it offers good budget accommodation as well as extensive logistic support. A 40-minute walk takes one up to the Pemayangtse *gompa* *(see page 78-79)*, one of the most important monasteries of Sikkim. Spend the day observing the rhythms of an ancient religion before heading back to Pelling.

Day 2: Pelling to Sangacholing

The trail westward to Sangacholing *gompa* is well worn and 45 minutes will bring one to this monastery which is older even than Pemayangtse *(see page 85)*. Return to Pelling for the night.

Day 3: Pelling to Khechopalri Lake and Monastery

By road, the sacred lake is a good 27 kms away but the trekking trail is shorter, though steeper. Close to five hours of walking will get you to this placid lake and the monastery is another half hour's trek away. There is a trekkers' hut, as well as a pilgrim's hut at the Lake, and the few villagers in the area are also willing to put tourists up.

Day 4: Khechopalri to Dubdi via Yuksam

The trail to Yuksam heads downhill for the first two hours and then climbs gradually.

From Yuksam, the Dubdi monastery *(see page 86)* is another hour's walk. Return to Yuksam for the night as there are a number of privately-owned hotels as well as a couple of government tourist bungalows here.

Day 5: Yuksam to Tashiding

Follow the road to Tashiding, where the monastery is a 45 minute hike up a conical hill between the Rangeet and Rathong rivers. It will take you the best part of a day's walking to get there, so stay the night at any of the small hotels.

Day 6: Tashiding to Legship

The walk down is an hour's work, from where one can take a jeep or bus back to Pelling.

Green Lake Trek

Falling as it does completely within restricted entry areas of North Sikkim, getting a permit for this trek is especially onerous. Best appraoach a travel agent with plenty of time in hand to complete the formalities.

Day 1: Lachen – Jakthang

The trek starts from the little town of Lachen, at an altitude of 2,700 metres and some 125 kms away from Gangtok. It is best to go along the highway to Thangu, 28 kms away. Keep heading north past the confluence of the Zemu and Lachen rivers; and then follow the Zemu Chu upstream through its forested valley heavy undergrowth.

Trek on until you cross the Lhonak river and reach Jakthang (3,300 metres) where a yak-herder's hut provides basic accommodation for the night.

Day 2: Jakthang – Yabuk

Yabuk is at the mouth of the Zemu Glacier and the 500 metre climb from Jakthang takes the good part of four hours. It is suggested that you don't push on to the Sona Camp the same day because it might bring on an attack of high altitude sickness.

Day 3 : Yabuk – Sona Camp

Follow the Zemu Glacier upwards and take care while negotiating the moraines and boulders. Attaining the Sona Camp at 4,500 metres is remarkable for the magnificent unhindred view it offers of the needlepoint Siniolchu, held by many to be the most beautiful peak in the world. The going will be slow here because the rarified air has little to offer.

Day 4: Sona Camp – Green Lake

This day's trek is made in full view of some of the most imposing mountains of the world – Siniolchu, Twins, Nepal Peak and Khang-chen-dzonga. The sight of the white peaks comes as a blessing despite the day's arduous walk. The Green Lake is a crystal body on the far east of the stretching plain, almost at the feet of the mighty K.

Day 5: Green Lake – Yabuk

Most people try to make this stretch downhill in a single day.

Day 6: Yabuk – Zema

Walk through the forest until Jakthang and then shadow the road until Zema from where one can hitch a ride back to Lachen.

Rhododendron Trek

(Season: March-May)

The base for this trek are the twin towns of Jorethang and Nayabazar, from where one can reach Hilley by bus via Sonbaria.

Day 1: Hilley to Versay

A four km walk from Hilley (2,743 metres) takes one to Versay (3,079 metres). The route winds through forests of silver fir, hemlock, magnolia and rhododendron, but as one nears Versay, the rhododendron edges other trees out of sight. A spring trek is a treat, with the trees glowing in shades of red. Versay has a tourist lodge for overnight stay, as well as a trekkers' hut.

Day 2: Versay to Dentam

Day 3: Dentam to Pemayangtse

Day 4: Pemayangtse to Versay

Day 5: Versay to Nayabazar

Other Trekking Routes

- Rumtek - Sang - Yangang - Ravangla - Tashiding - Yuksam
- Uttarey - Chiwabhanjang - Sikkim Megu - Datey Bhir - Gomuthang - Boktok - Thesaypla - Bikbari - Dzongri
- Namchi - Tendong - Damthang - Ravangla - Maenam - Bhaley Dhunga - Yangang - Sinchuthang - Bermoik - Namchi

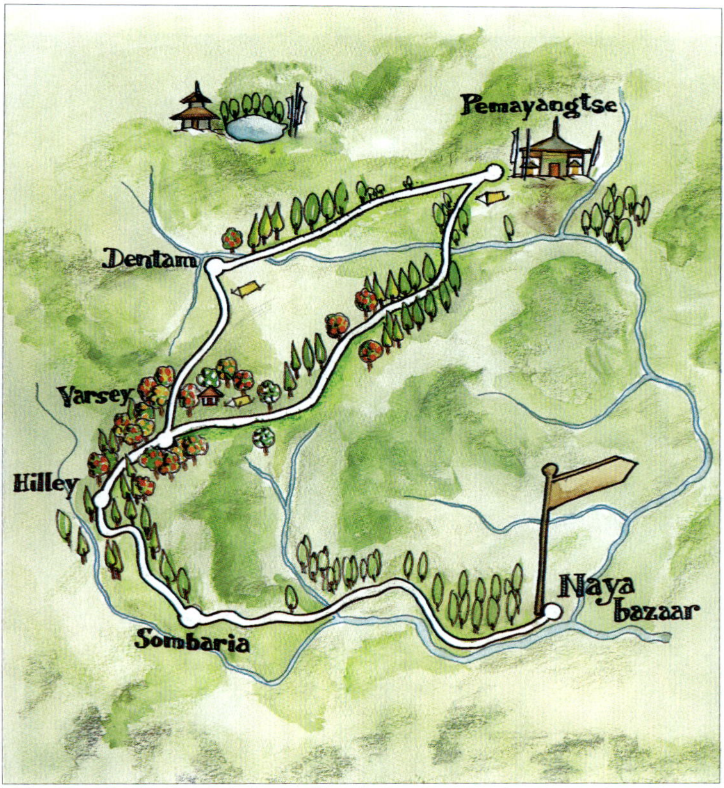

Mountaineering

Booking for Peaks
Mountain peaks can be booked for climbing through the Indian Mountaineering Foundation,
Benito Juarez Road,
New Delhi-110001
Phone: 4671211
Fax: 6883412
E-mail: indmount@del2.vsnl.net.in

You can choose the peak you want to climb in Sikkim from the list of peaks available with Survey of India. A peak has to be booked before an expedition begins climbing it.

Indian Mountaineering Foundation (IMF) is the apex body that conducts mountaineering expeditions and regulates climbing activities, makes bookings, and monitors the progress of expeditions. It also broadcasts weather bulletins on the state-owned All-India Radio. In case of accidents, it conducts search, rescue and evacuation operations.

Booking for a peak should be made well in advance, as there is a waiting period of almost two years for the more popular peaks. While booking you must give names of two alternative peaks. In case the peak you want to climb is not available, IMF can book another peak for you. If you want to climb a peak in the restricted area, you must name some peaks lying in the open area as alternatives.

Below: Khang-chen-dzonga as seen from Pelling

You must deal only with operators and agencies recognised by government tourism departments and affiliated to IMF. You can obtain this list from IMF.

Mountaineering equipment can be hired from IMF through their store in Delhi. It is open on all working days between 10 am and 5 pm. For mountaineering in Sikkim, the Himalayan Mountaineering Institute in Darjeeling is another place to hire equipment. However, it is best to bring your own equipment as the security charges in India are very high. Equipment brought into India by foreign expeditions is exempt from custom duty, provided the IMF officially authorises it.

Two peaks in West Sikkim, Thingchen Khang and Jopunob have been declared trekking peaks (peaks under 6,000 metres are generally termed as trekking peaks) which means they are exempt from the royalty for climbing. They can be climbed with the usual trekking permits.

SANCTUARIES	AREA	HEIGHT	SEASON	DISTANCE
Khang-chen-dzonga National Park	1,729 sq kms		Apr-Aug, Oct-Dec	142 kms from Gangtok
Kyongnosla Alpine Sanctuary	31 sq kms	3,200-4,100 metres.	Apr-Aug, Oct-Nov	31 kms from Gangtok
Maenam Sanctuary	35 sq kms	2,155 metres	Mar-May, Sept-Nov	Ravangla the starting point is 24 kms short of Legship
Singba Rhododendron Sanctuary	43 sq kms		Mar-May	149 kms from Gangtok
Versay Rhododendron Sanctuary		3,700 metres	Mar-May	
Fambong La Reserve	52 sq kms	upto 2,187 metres	Mar-May, Sept-Dec	21 kms from Gangtok

FLORA	FAUNA	LODGING	FEE	
Pine, oak, chestnut, rhododendrons and giant magnolias	Himalayan brown bear, black bear, snow leopard, musk deer, flying squirrel, red panda and some 600 species of birds.	Trekkers' Huts at Yuksam	Rs 150 for trekkers, pack animals etc. extra Rs 100	
Juniper and silver firs; orchids and rhododendrons, primulas, blue poppies, clematis and many plants useful in Tibetan medicine.	Himalayan marmot, goral, serow, red panda, Himalayan black bear, Tibetan fox, yellow-throated martens, musk deer and colourful pheasants	Two-roomed log huts available at Kyangnosla and Manilakhang	Rs 5	
Bamboo trees; magnolia and rhododendrons	Red panda, civet, blood pheasant, black eagle, magpie, sun-birds			
Several alpine varieties of tree; varieties of rhododendron	Tiger-civet and birds like blood pheasant, partridge			For further details of entry fee and lodging facilities contact – Sikkim Tourism, M G Road, Gangtok. Phone: 22634, 20352
Oak and magnolia trees; 10-15 species of rhododendrons				
	Himalayan black bear, red panda, civet			For permits contact – Chief Wildlife Warden, Sikkim Forest Department, Deorali, Gangtok Phone: 80191

The Kerang Plateau in North Sikkim is one of the
most rugged areas of the state

PRACTICAL INFORMATION

Sikkim is beautiful any time of the year – whether draped in winter white, bedecked in spring flowers or even wreathed in a monsoon haze. For trekkers and travellers, however, perhaps it is best to visit either between end-March and mid-May or later, between October and early December.

The spring season is best to catch the flowers, orchids and rhododendrons alike. And the winter months are best for mountain viewing as the monsoons have cleared the atmosphere.

WHAT TO WEAR

It can get very chilly in Sikkim and a heavy pullover or a light jacket are needed even in the summer evenings. An umbrella in the monsoon or a waterproof anorak are not just wise but necessary. While visiting the *gompas* be dressed decorously; women should avoid going in shorts or halter-neck blouses.

BEFORE COMING TO INDIA

There are a few things you need to take care of before travelling to India.

Visa

There are three kinds of visas for tourists.

- The 15-day single / double-entry transit visa. This visa is valid for 30 days from the date of its issue.
- The 3-month multiple-entry visa. This visa is valid for 90 days from the date of first entry into India, which must be within 30 days from the date of its issue.
- The 6-month multiple-entry visa. This visa is valid for 180 days from the date of its issue, not from the date of entry into India.

Visa Extension

It is virtually impossible to get the 15-day or 3-month visa extended. Only the 6-month tourist visa can be extended. It can be quite a bother to extend it beyond a 15-day period. Avoid it unless there is an emergency.

A 15-day extension on the 6-month visa is issued by the Foreigner's Regional Registration Office (FRRO) at any of the four metros: Delhi, Kolkata, Chennai, Mumbai. The FRRO office is open on weekdays, 9.30 am to 1.30 pm and 2 pm to 4 pm. A l5-day extension is given only if confirmed air tickets are not available. No fee is charged.

- **Chennai**
  Shastri Bhawan Annexe
  26 Haddows Road, Nungambakkam
  Ph 044-8240338
- **Kolkata**
  237 A J C Bose Road
  Ph 033-2470549
- **Mumbai**
  Annexe-II, Crawford Market
  (near Police Commissioner's Office)
  Ph 022-2621169
- **New Delhi**
  East Block 8, Level-II
  Sector-I, R K Puram
  Ph 011-6711443 / 384 / 074

Travel Insurance

Take a travel insurance policy, covering theft and loss, before coming to India. Also buy a medical insurance.

There are several kinds of insurance policies. Make the right choice after consulting a reliable travel agent in your country.

Health

Your health during your travel in India depends on three things: Precautions taken before arrival, day-to-day health care, and efficiency in tackling emergencies.

No particular vaccination is required for coming to India. However, visitors from designated countries in Africa, South America and Papua New Guinea, even if they are on transit, are required to bring valid Yellow Fever vaccination certificates. In the absence of this certificate they will be quarantined for six days.

Precautionary medication is the best bet against common ailments like diarrhoea, dysentry and malaria. Malaria is a problem in India during the rainy season. So, if you are coming at that time of the year, do consult your doctor for precautionary anti-malarial medication. While in India, use mosquito repellent ointment.

If you are not already vaccinated against hepatitis B, get it done before travelling.

Those not accustomed to Indian conditions are usually vulnerable to stomach problems. It is advisable to seek medical advice before travelling and carry your own first-aid kit.

For travel health, use your common sense. Take care of what you eat or drink. This is the most important health rule. Water is suspect, therefore, it is best to carry your own mineral water. Bottled mineral water and aerated drinks are easily available and are a good substitute for water. Hot tea and coffee are also good alternatives.

Hospitals

Indian cities have government as well as privately run hospitals and nursing homes. The government hospitals have modern medical facilities but due to large patient turnout, medical assistance is slow.

Things you can bring into India

Visitors can bring in articles for personal use, including cameras with five rolls of film, a reasonable quantity of jewellery, a pair of binoculars, a portable musical instrument, a portable radio, a tape recorder, a portable typewriter, a laptop computer and professional equipment. On arrival, you will have to give an undertaking on a Tourist Baggage Re-Export (TBRE) form, available with Customs officials at the Airport, that you will take these items back when you leave. This form, along with the articles that are entered in it, have to be shown to the Customs officials at the time of departure.

Designated 'high-value articles' are also allowed in, but on a written undertaking that they will be taken back at the time of departure. Please obtain a Landing Certificate if you are expecting unaccompanied baggage and for mishandled baggage.

You can bring in 200 cigarettes (or 50 cigars or 250 gms of tobacco) and liquor and wines up to 32 oz (1 litre).

You are allowed to bring in any amount of foreign currency in cash or travellers' cheques. However, if you are carrying more than US $ 2,500 (or equivalent), you have to declare it on arrival. Fill up the Currency Declaration Form (CDF) which is to be attested by the Customs Officer. Indian currency cannot be brought in nor taken out of the country.

Things you can take Back

Export Regulations

A visitor can take back the following goods:
(A) Souvenirs (including Indian silk, wool, handicrafts, etc.) without any limit.
(B) Gold jewellery and silverware up to a value of Rs100,000 (and in excess of that only after obtaining a permit from the RBI, the Indian central bank).
(C) Other jewellery and precious stones, but if of high value, these should be appraised by the Customs Appraiser at the airport before departure. As a general rule, get an RBI permit for goods of high value. There are restrictions on the export of antiques and art objects which are more than 100 years old. In case of doubt, consult the Director, Antiquities, Archaeological Survey of India Janpath, New Delhi (Ph 011-3017443). It is also advisable to get a certificate of proof.

Export of most wildlife products is either prohibited or strictly regulated. Do not buy articles made of ivory, reptile, tiger or deer skin, tortoise shell, shahtoosh shawls made by killing the Tibetan antelope.

Tax Clearance Certificate

If you stay in India for more than 120 days (four months), from the date of issue of the visa, regardless of your date of entry into India, you would be required to furnish a tax clearance certificate to leave the country. This is to prove that you did not earn money while in India and that your trip was financed with the money brought in. If you are planning to stay in India for more than four months, be careful with your documents relating to travel finance.

Customs

There are two channels for customs clearance at International terminals in Indian airports: Green Channel and Red Channel.
Green Channel: This is for unihindered exit from the airport. You can walk through the Green Channel if you are not carrying goods which attract customs duty.
Red Channel: For those who have anything to declare, including money worth more than US $2,500.

Foreign Travel Tax

Rs 500 has to be paid at the airport as Foreign Travel Tax when leaving the country. For travel to Pakistan, Nepal, Sri Lanka, Bhutan, Myanmar, the Maldives and Afghanistan, the tax is Rs 150.

Arriving in India by Air

You can touchdown in India at the international airports in any of the four metropolitan cities, Chennai, Delhi, Kolkata and Mumbai. Most international airlines fly to India from virtually every continent. For travellers heading for Sikkim, it might be best to take either Delhi or Kolkata as your entry-point.

Delhi

The Delhi airport is called the Indira Gandhi International Airport. It has two terminals: Terminal 1 (domestic) and Terminal 2 (international). The two terminals are 7 kms away from each other. Terminal 2 is located about 19 kms from the city centre (Connaught Place).

Airport Enquiry
Domestic Terminal
Ph 5675121/ 5675126
International Terminal
Ph 5652011/ 5652021

Airlines Offices

- **Indian Airlines**
Malhotra Building
F Block, Connaught Place
City Office Ph 3310517
Airport 5675121
- **Jet Airways**
N 40 Connaught Place
City Office Ph 3321241
Airport 5675404
- **Sahara India Airlines**
Ambadeep Building
14 K G Marg
City Office Ph 3326851
Airport 5675234
- **Air India**
Jeevan Bharti Building
124 Connaught Circus
City Office Ph 3731225
Airport 5696621

Khang-chen-dzonga viewed from Dzongri

Tourist Information Offices
- **Tourist Office**
Government of India
88 Janpath, New Delhi
Ph 3320008
- **Sikkim Tourism**
14 Panchsheel Marg Chanakyapuri,
New Delhi
Ph 6881976

Kolkata

The Kolkata airport is called Netaji Subhash Chandra Bose Airport, and is 22 kms from the city centre. It has two terminals, International and Domestic located in the same building.

Airlines Offices
- **Indian Airlines**
City Office Ph 2360730.
Airport Ph 5119637
- **Jet Airways**
City Office Ph 2292227.
Airport Ph 5118836
- **Sahara India Airlines**
City Office Ph 2827686.
Airport Ph 5119545
- **Air India**
City Office Ph 2822356.
Airport Ph 5119864

Tourist Information Offices
Tourist Office,
Government of India
4 Shakespeare Sarani
Ph 2421402, 2421475

TRAVEL WITHIN INDIA

By Air

There are several airlines that fly to domestic destinations. The biggest is the Indian Airlines, a state-owned domestic carrier. Other major flyers are Jet Airways and Sahara India Airlines.

Hand Baggage

In all domestic flights, passengers are allowed one piece of hand baggage. All baggage is subject to security check whether carried by hand or booked in the hold.

Baggage Allowance

Domestic airlines allow 20 kgs check-in baggage for Economy Class and 30 kgs for Business Class. Excess baggage is charged as per the schedule available at the airlines counter.

The reporting time for all domestic flights is 60 minutes prior to departure.

By Rail

The Indian Railways run a gigantic, modern and organised network which connects the metros to most major and minor destinations within India.

Ticket Reservation

Trains in India are very crowded and it is necessary to reserve a seat or a berth to travel in any degree of comfort.

Rail reservations start from 60 days before the date of travel. Reservations can be cancelled up to 24 hours before the train leaves, but a nominal cancellation fee has to be paid.

Train tickets must be bought before you enter the train. You will be penalised if you do not have one and intend to buy it on board.

International Travel Bureau

The Bureau on the first floor of New Delhi railway station has a special booking office for foreigners. It is open Monday through Saturday, 7.30 am to 5 pm. Tickets here are issued only to foreign nationals and non-resident Indians against payment in US dollars. Such tickets get a priority on reservation under the Foreign Tourist Quota and are exempted from reservation fees.

MONEY

Indian Currency

Indian currency is called the Rupee. It is available in denominations of 1000, 500, 100, 50, 20, 10, 5, 2, 1. One rupee equals 100 paise. Coins in common use are those of Rs 5, Rs 2 , Re 1 and 50 and 25 paise. The 20, 10 and 5 paise coins have become redundant in big cities, but they still have value in smaller towns and in rural India. Be careful not to accept soiled notes.

Credit Cards

Credit cards are becoming increasingly popular in urban areas. All major international credit cards are used, Visa, Amex, Mastercard.

Banks

Banks are open from 10 am to 2 pm Monday to Friday and 10 am to 12 pm Saturdays. Banks are closed on Sundays and national holidays. Most international banks have branches in major cities.

Tips or Baksheesh

There is no rule which compels you to tip anyone for any service rendered. Courtesy demands that you tip a waiter in a restaurant or hotel. The general norm is to pay 10 per cent of the billed amount. Taxis, auto rickshaws, public transport staff, government officials or private service providers are not expected to be tipped. It is entirely up to you to tip someone for services rendered. Sometimes the urge to tip can be misunderstood, as it may be considered an assault on personal dignity.

COMMUNICATIONS

Post Offices

The main post offices in large towns provide a wide range of facilities, like telegraph, fax and a courier service which operates under the brand name EMS-Speed Post.

If you need to dispatch a letter or document urgently it might be advisable to send it by the government-run Speed Post.

Parcels by mail should not exceed 20 kgs. Books, documents, papers and printed material can be sent by book post which costs less.

All Post Offices are open from 10 am to 6 pm Monday to Saturday.

Telephone

ISD (international), STD (domestic long distance), and local telephone booths are available all over India.

The rates for international calls are fixed, but calls within the country are charged on the basis of a pulse rate which varies for different cities, and for different times of the day.

Most booths remain open till midnight. Some of these booths have facilities for sending and receiving fax messages.

Email

Internet and email connections are easily available from anywhere in India. Gangtok, too, has innumerable cybercafes, where for a nominal amount you can access the net.

Police Assistance Booths

Police assistance booths are located at the airports, railway stations and near the major bus stops.

Lost Articles

In case of loss or theft, especially vital documents like passports, an FIR (First Information Report) must be filed at the Police Station nearest to the place where the loss occurred. In case of loss of documents the embassy or high commission concerned must be immediately informed.

EMBASSIES & HIGH COMMISSIONS IN NEW DELHI

Afghanistan
5/50 F Shanti Path
Chanakyapuri
Ph 6883601-02
Fax 6875439
Mumbai (022) 3633777

Australia
1/50 G Shanti Path
Chanakyapuri
Ph 6888223, 6885556
Fax 6874126
Chennai (044) 5342705
Kolkata (033) 4763768
Mumbai (022) 2181071/72

Austria
EP 13 Chandragupta Marg
Chanakyapuri
Ph 6889050, 6889049
Fax 6886929
Chennai (044) 8278739
Kolkata (033) 2871760/61
Mumbai (022) 2874758/59

Bangladesh
56 Ring Road
Lajpat Nagar III
Ph 6834668/6839209
Fax 6840596
Kolkata (033) 2475208

Belgium
50 N Shanti Path
Chanakyapuri
Ph 6875728
Fax 6885821
Chennai (044) 2352336
Kolkata (033) 2827531
Mumbai (022)4955186

Bhutan
Chandragupta Marg
Chanakyapuri
Ph 6889230
Fax 6876710
Kolkata (033) 2473159

Canada
7/8 Shanti Path
Chanakyapuri
Ph 6876500 Fax 6876579
Chennai (044) 4767818
Kolkata (033) 2208515
Mumbai (022) 2876027-30

China
50 D Shanti Path
Chanakyapuri
Ph 6871586
Fax 6885486
Mumbai (022) 4915861-62

Denmark
11 Aurangzeb Road
Ph 3010900
Fax 3792019
Chennai (044) 8118140
Kolkata (033) 2487476
Mumbai (022) 2618181

Finland
E 3 Nyaya Marg
Chanakaypuri
Ph 6115258
Fax 6886713
Chennai (044) 8523622
Kolkata (033) 2474328
Mumbai (022) 2165277

France
2/50 E Shanti Path
Chanakyapuri
Ph 6118790
Fax 6872305
Kolkata (033) 4791141-42
Mumbai (022) 4950918

Germany
6/50 G Shanti Path
Chanakyapuri
Ph 6871831
Fax 6877623
Chennai (044) 8271747
Kolkata (033) 4791141
Mumbai (022) 2832422

Greece
EP 32
Dr Radhakrisnan Marg
Chanakyapuri
Ph 6880700
Fax 6888010
Chennai (044) 8200042
Mumbai (022) 6607431

Indonesia
50 A Kautilya Marg
Chanakyapuri
Ph 6118642, 6118646
Fax 6874402
Chennai (044) 4942020
Kolkata (033) 2102653, 2102679
Mumbai (022) 3868678, 3800940

Iran
5 Barakhamba Road
Ph 3329600
Fax 3354093
Mumbai (022) 3630073, 3634102

Ireland
13 Jor Bagh
Ph 4626714, 462633
Fax 4697053
Mumbai (022) 2872045
Bangalore (080) 8523425

Israel
3 Aurangzeb Road
Ph 3013238
Fax 3014298
Kolkata (033) 2880040
Mumbai (022) 2819993

Italy
50 E Chandragupta Marg
Chanakyapuri
Ph 6114355
Fax 6873889
Kolkata (033) 4792426
Mumbai (022) 3804071

Japan
50 G Shanti Path
Chanakyapuri
Ph 6876581
Fax 6885587
Chennai (044) 4323860
Kolkata (033) 4211970
Mumbai (022) 4933857

Kenya
66 Vasant Marg
Vasant Vihar
Ph 6146538
Fax 6146550

Kuwait
5 A Shanti Path
Chanakyapuri
Ph 4100791
Fax 6873516
Mumbai (O22) 2871897

Malaysia
50 M Satya Marg
Chanakyapuri
Ph 6111291-92
Fax 6881538
Chennai (O44) 4343048

Mauritius
5 Kautilya Marg
Chanakyapuri
Ph 4102161 Fax 4102194
Chennai (044) 2346693
Mumbai (022) 2845466-67
Kolkata (033) 2480114

Mexico
26 D Sardar Patel Marg,
Chanakyapuri
Ph 4107182-84
Fax 4107185

Myanmar
3/50 F Nyaya Marg
Chanakyapuri
Ph 6889007 Fax 6877942

Nepal
1 Barakhamba Road
Ph 3329218
Fax 3326857
Kolkata (033) 4791117

New Zealand
50 N Nyaya Marg
Chanakyapuri
Ph 6883170
Fax 6872317
Chennai (044) 8112472

Nigeria
21 Olof Palme Marg
Vasant Vihar
Ph 6146221 Fax 6146641

Norway
50 C Shanti Path
Chanakyapuri
Ph 6873573, 6873532
Fax 6873814
Chennai (044) 5245314
Kolkata (033) 2478804
Mumbai (022) 2842042

Pakistan
2/50 G Shanti Path
Chanakyapuri
Ph 6110601, 6110605
Fax 6872339

Philippines
50 N Nyaya Marg
Chanakyapuri
Ph 4101120, 6889091
Fax 6876401
Chennai (044) 2354063, 2352062
Kolkata (033) 2808353
Mumbai (022) 4792202, 2024792

Portugal
8 Olof Palme Marg
Vasant Vihar
Ph 6142212, 6142215
Fax 6152837
Goa (0832) 224004
Kolkata (033) 4499700

Russia
Shanti Path
Chanakyapuri
Ph 6873800
Fax 6876823
Chennai (044) 4982330
Kolkata (033) 4797006
Mumbai (022) 3633628

Saudi Arabia
D12 NDSE II
Ph 6256419
Fax 6257082
Mumbai (022) 2182619, 2187768

Singapore
E 6 Chandragupta Marg
Chanakyapuri
Ph 6885659
Fax 6886798
Chennai (044) 8470544
Kolkata (033) 2823820
Mumbai (022) 2043205

South Africa
B 18 Vasant Marg
Vasant Vihar
Ph 6149411
Fax 6143605
Kolkata (033) 2400950, 2474107
Mumbai (022) 3893725, 3893729

South Korea
9 Chandragupta Marg
Chanakyapuri
Ph 6885374, 6885376
Fax 6884840
Chennai (044) 8237307 (Telefax)
Kolkata (033) 2485102-05
Mumbai (022) 3886743-45

Spain
16 Sunder Nagar
Ph 4359004, 4359567
Fax 4359008
Chennai (044) 4942008
Kolkata (033) 4695954
Mumbai (022) 2835232

Sri Lanka
27 Kautilya Marg
Chanakyapuri
Ph 3010201
Fax 3793604
Chennai (044) 4987896
Kolkata (033) 2210005
Mumbai (022) 2045861

Sweden
Nyaya Marg
Chanakyapuri
Ph 4197100
Fax 6885401
Chennai (044) 8271747
Kolkata (033) 4792414
Mumbai (022) 3804071

Switzerland
Nyaya Marg
Chanakyapuri
Ph 6878372
Fax 6873093
Chennai (044) 4332701
Kolkata (033) 2295542-43
Mumbai (022) 2884563

Thailand
56 N Nyaya Marg
Chanakyapuri
Ph 6118103
Fax 6872029
Kolkata (033) 4403230-31
Mumbai (022) 3631404

The Netherlands
6/50 F Shanti Path
Chanakyapuri
Ph 6884951
Fax 6884956
Chennai (044) 4473309
Kolkata (033) 2424979
Mumbai (022) 2016750

Turkey
50 N Nyaya Marg
Chanakyapuri
Ph 6889054
Fax 6881409

U A E
12 Chandragupta Marg
Chanakyapuri
Ph 6872937, 6872822
Fax 6873272
Mumbai (022) 2183021, 2345566

United Kingdom
Shanti Path
Chanakyapuri
Ph 6872161
Fax 4670234
Chennai (044) 8273136-37
Kolkata (033) 2885172
Mumbai (022) 2830517

United States of America
21 Shanti Path
Chanakyapuri
Ph 4198000
Fax 4190017
Chennai (044) 8112000
Kolkata (033) 2825757
Mumbai (022) 3633611

STD Codes:
New Delhi 011
Chennai 044
Kolkata 033
Mumbai 022

ENTRY PERMITS FOR SIKKIM

As a border state, Sikkim has some entry and travel restrictions. All foreign tourists are required to get a 15-day permit known as the Inner Line Permit (ILP) before they can travel in Sikkim.

But don't let that daunt you. The permits can be acquired within minutes at a number of places (see list below), including the Indian mission in your home country. All that is needed is that you provide two passport-sized photographs and copies of your passport and the Indian visa.

These permits, valid for all sub-divisions in Sikkim apart from Chungthang sub-division of North Sikkim, can also be obtained from the Sikkim Tourism offices in New Delhi, Kolkata or Siliguri.

In fact, don't despair even if you find yourself heading for Sikkim without an inner line permit; you can get one at Rangpo, the entry point into the hill state. Contact the tourist officer at the Rangpo Tourist Centre who will issue a two-day permit which can then be extended for 15 days at Gangtok.

The 15-day permit can again be extended thrice for periods of 15 days at any of the addresses listed below:

- **Foreigners' Regional Registration** Office in Chennai, Kolkata, Mumbai, and New Delhi
- **Immigration officers** at the airports in Chennai, Kolkata, Mumbai and New Delhi
- **Resident Commissioner**
  Government of Sikkim
  New Sikkim House
  14 Panchsheel Marg
  Chanakyapuri
  New Delhi Ph 6113747
- **Asst. Resident Commissioner**
  Government of Sikkim
  4/1 Middleton Street
  Kolkata Ph 2815328

On the road to Yumthang

- **Chief Secretary or Home Secretary**
  Government of Sikkim
  Tashiling Secretariat
  Gangtok Ph 22315, 24323
- **Director General of Police**
  Government of Sikkim
  Gangtok Ph 22341, 22747
- **Deputy Director (Tourism)**
  Government of Sikkim
  SNT Colony
  Hill Cart Road
  Siliguri Ph -432646

After obtaining the permit, foreign tourists, individuals as well as groups, can visit major tourist destinations of Sikkim, including Gangtok, Rumtek, Pemayangtse, and Phodong.

For both foreign as well as domestic tourists, travel to areas beyond Chungthang – and this includes the Lachen and Lachung Valleys, Yumthang, and Gurudongmar Lake – is even more restricted and requires a Protected Area Permit. Tourists can only go there under the aegis of a travel agent sponsored by the Government of Sikkim.

Foreigners also need this Protected Area Permit to travel to the higher reaches of West Sikkim – including portions of the Dzongri trekking trail – and to the Tsomgo Lake east of Gangtok. So, for anything beyond the beaten track of Gangtok, Rumtek and Pemayangtse, it is best to go through a reputed travel agent.

Areas other than those mentioned above can also be visited, but the special permit required for these is relatively difficult to get, and can be obtained only from the Ministry of Home Affairs, North Block, New Delhi.

STD Codes:
East Sikkim/North Sikkim 03592
West Sikkim/South Sikkim 03595
Siliguri/Bagdogra 0353

GETTING TO SIKKIM

BY AIR

Sikkim is not directly linked by air. The nearest airport is at Bagdogra in the northern part of the state of West Bengal. India's state-run carrier, Indian Airlines, as well as other private airline services have several flights linking Bagdogra to Guwahati, Kolkata and New Delhi daily.

Timings and fares of flights are liable to change on short notice; please check with your travel agent or the airline office for the updated information.

Helicopter Service

There is also a helicopter service connecting Bagdogra to Gangtok, which takes about 30 minutes to reach Gangtok and costs Rs 1,500 per head. The helicopter can take five persons per trip. Contact Travel Service Agency, Pradhan Nagar, Siliguri. Ph (0353)-531219 and (0353)-551036 in Bagdogra. The service operates in all seasons.

STDC also organises helicopter sightseeing tours from Gangtok that give you an aerial view of Sikkim's natural beauty. For bookings contact Sikkim Tourism, M G Marg, Gangtok, Ph (03592) 22634, 22413.

Flight Connections

	Flt No.
Delhi-Bagdogra	IC 789, IC 879 9W 601, 9W 601
Kolkata-Bagdogra	IC 721, IC 721, 9W 617
Bagdogra-Delhi	IC 7892, IC 879 9W 601/2
Bagdogra-Kolkata	IC 722, IC 721 9W 618, IC 879, 9W 601/2, 9W 602

Airline Offices

Indian Airlines
Hotel Mainak
Hill Cart Road
Siliguri
City Office Ph (0353)-431495, 511495 Fax 431509
Airport Ph (0353)-551666, 551192

Jet Airways
Hotel Vinayak
Hill Cart Road
Siliguri
City Office Ph (0353)-435876, 435877, 538001
Airport Ph (0353)-551588-90

By Rail

Sikkim's nearest railhead is at New Jalpaiguri or NJP (124 kms from Gangtok), the railway junction attached to the West Bengal town of Siliguri . Most domestic tourists headed for Sikkim take advantage of the fact that

Train Connections

Delhi-NJP*-Delhi	
Mahananda Exp	Daily
Avadh Assam Exp	Daily
North East Exp	Daily
Rajdhani Exp	Mon, Fri
Rajdhani Exp	Tue, Wed, Sat
Rajdhani Exp	Mon, Thu, Fri
Rajdhani Exp	Wed, Sun
Kolkata-NJP-Kolkata	
Testa Torsa Exp	Daily
Darjeeling Mail	Daily
Kanchanjanga Exp	Daily
Kamrup Exp	Daily

*NJP: New Jalpaiguri

New Jalpaiguri is one of the best connected junctions in the country, with daily trains to Delhi, Kolkata and other major towns and cities.

BY ROAD

The second lap of the journey to Sikkim, from Bagdogra or Siliguri onward, has to be completed by road. It is a 124-km journey to Gangtok, the Sikkimese capital, and the run takes approximately five hours. Private taxis or jeeps can be hired at Bagdogra airport for the drive to Sikkim. Sikkim Nationalised Transport (SNT) also runs a daily bus service from Gangtok, the state capital, direct to Bagdogra airport.

It is best to take a taxi or auto-rickshaw from Bagdogra airport into Siliguri town some 12 kms away. From there, buses of the Sikkim Nationalised Transport leave for various destinations. You can book a seat in advance by calling the SNT Booking Office in Siliguri, Ph (0353) 421496, 43275.

Several private-run buses also ply between Siliguri and the major towns of Sikkim, including Gangtok and Jorethang. These buses can be boarded at the Tenzing Norgay Bus Stand, Ph (0353) 514920.

The major diversion on the drive up to Gangtok – besides, of course, the stunning scenery – are the road signs put up by the Border Roads' Organisation (BRO). The yellow signboards along the verge carry pithy sayings ranging from the clever ('Better to be late Mr Driver than The Late Mr Driver') through the sentimental ('BRO – Cutting Hills but Joining Hearts') to the downright salacious ('Be gentle on my curves').

Private cars can be hired on a full-use or share basis. The share-cabs can be taken from outside the SNT office in Siliguri. The journey into the terraced green of Sikkim is a refreshing experience in itself.

GANGTOK

Gangtok, the capital of Sikkim is located in the East district of Sikkim. It became the capital city only in the 1800s. It is not a picturesque town in its architecture, but its location on a ridge is unsurpassable. The city offers spectacular views of the snow-clad Khang-chen-dzonga range. Over the past few years, Gangtok has emerged as a popular hill station.

Air Bookings

For Indian Airlines' and Jet Airways' bookings in Gangtok, contact:

Josse & Josse
Ph 24682, 25534

RNC Enterprises
Ph 28652, 28653

Silk Route Tours & Travels
Ph 23354, 29150

By Road

Gangtok is connected by road to Darjeeling, Kalimpong, Siliguri. The Sikkim Nationalised Transport (SNT) runs regular bus services from Gangtok to all towns in Sikkim as well as to the major cities of north Bengal. Private taxis are available at Bagdogra and Siliguri for Gangtok and the run from Bagdogra to Gangtok costs about Rs 250 per head.

Travel Around Sikkim

Jeep/Car

The best way to travel from point to point in Sikkim is by Jeep. More comfortable than the always over-crowded buses and much faster, these are easily available in the city.

Important Road Distances

Bagdogra – Gangtok	124 km
Nathula – Gangtok	56 km
Namchi Bazaar – Gangtok	79 km
Gangtok – Pelling	117 km
Gangtok – Rangpo	40 km
Gangtok – Rumtek	24 km
Gangtok – Tsomgo Lake	40 km
Gangtok – Yumthang	140 km
Yuksam – Pemayangtse	32 km

Jeeps and cars for hire can also be shared and the cost split. The rates for various destinations are fixed and are followed religiously.

- For Siliguri, Darjeeling and Kalimpong – from Private Bus Stand.
- For Pemayangtse, Pelling and other places in West Sikkim – from Children's Park.
- For Phodong, Yumthang and Chungthang in North Sikkim – from Children's Park.
- For Rumtek – from Lall Market.

Rail Bookings

Railway bookings for journeys onward from New Jalpaiguri can be made in Gangtok at the counter in the SNT Bus Stand. Ph 22014, 22634, 22413

Bus

State-run SNT buses connect all corners of Sikkim. Booking facilities for the state-run SNT buses are available at the SNT Bus Stand on Paljor Stadium Road, Ph 22016, but most hotels can also help. Private buses leave from Private Bus Stand on NH31A, Ph 22856.

Sikkim Tourism Offices

Bagdogra
Sikkim Tourist Information Counter
Bagdogra Airport
Ph (0353) 551036

Gangtok
Sikkim Tourist Information Centre
Ph (03592) 21634, 23425

Kolkata
Sikkim Tourist Information Centre
Sikkim House
4/1 Middleton Street
Ph (033) 2815328, 2468983

New Delhi
Sikkim Tourist Information Centre
New Sikkim House
14 Panchsheel Marg
Chanakyapuri
Ph (011) 6115346, 6115171, 6881976 extn 203

Rangpo
Tourist Information Centre
Ph (03592) 40818

Siliguri
Sikkim Tourist Information Centre
SNT Colony
Ph (0353) 432646

Foreigners' Regional Registration Office,
Kazi Road, Ph 23041

Travel & Trekking Agencies

Atlas Tours & Services
Super Market
Ph 20540, 25273

Bayul Tours & Treks
Super Market
Ph 28341, 21724

Blue Sky Tours & Travels
Tibet Road
Ph 23330, 25113

Denzong Adventure
Tibet Road
Ph 25558

Everest Tours & Treks
P S Road
Ph 24489, 22070

Himalayan Trekking
P N G Road
Ph 26518

Kanishka Travels
NH 31A
Ph 24011, 24690

Khangri Tours & Treks
Tibet Road
Ph 26050, 29851

Khorlo Tours & Travels
Tibet Road
Ph 25353, 20307

Marcopolo World Travels
P S Road
Ph 24116, 29407

Modern Treks & Tours
Tibet Road
Ph 26562, 27319

Namgyal Tour & Treks
Tibet Road
Ph 23701, 27027

Pardik Tours & Travels
M G Marg
Ph 22316, 23250

Potala Tours & Travels
P S Road
Ph 22041, 24434

RNC Enterprise
M G Marg
Ph 28652-53

Seven Seas Tours & Expeditions
P S Road
Ph 21740, 26980

Sikkim Adventure
6th Mile, Tadong
Ph 51706, 51250

Sikkim Tours & Travels
Church Road
Ph 22188, 27191

Sikkim Travel International
Near Star Cinema Hall
Ph 28335, 28338

Sikkim Treks & Travels
Development Area
Ph 23797, 26738

Sikkim World Expedition
Zero Point
23494, 20858

Silk Route Tours & Travels
M G Marg
Ph 23354, 29150

Sinolchu Tours & Treks
D P H Road
Ph 25569, 24572

Sony Tours & Travels
Metropoint
Ph 26490, 31997

Tashila Tours & Treks
NH 31A
Ph 22155, 22979

Tsozum Tours & Travels
Baluwakhani
Ph 24950

Vajra Adventure Tours
Arithang Road
Ph 22759

Wangchuk Travel Agency
P S Road
Ph 22446

Yak & Yeti Tours & Travels
NH 31A
Ph 21670, 20878

Yoksum Tours & Treks
Behind Telephone Exchange
Ph 23473, 26822

Yumthang Tours & Travels
Tibet Road
Ph 26276

Zambhala Tours & Treks
NH 31A
Ph 29651, 23753

Travel Agents' Association of Sikkim
Ph 20842

Banks

Bank of Baroda
M G Marg
Ph 23216

Bank of India
New Market
Ph 24388

Canara Bank
M G Marg
Ph 23589

Central Bank of India
P S Road
Ph 22649

Punjab National Bank
Deorali
Ph 80170

State Bank of India
M G Marg
Ph 26091, 22224

State Bank of Sikkim
NH 31A
Ph 22255

UCO Bank
PS Road
Ph 23164

Union Bank of India
Tibet Road

Vijaya Bank
Metropoint
Ph 22131

Book Shops

City News
M G Marg
Ph 25660

Jainco
NH 31A
Ph 23774

Moti Mahal
New Market
Ph 24330, 23998

Photo/Colour Labs

Color Calcutta
New Market

Multimedia
M G Marg
Ph 29897, 27062

New Studio
L M Road

Orient Studio
M G Marg
Ph 24114

Oswal Corporation
(Digital)
New Market
Ph 21477

Panorama Colour Lab
New Market
Ph 25098, 22488

Photomedia
New Market

Somani Colour Lab
New Market
Ph 23813

Tse Ten Tashi & Co
M G Marg

Tashi & Sons
L M Road

Foreign Exchange

Curio Craft Gallery
P S Road
Ph 25368, 25739

Silk Route Tours & Travels
M G Marg
Ph 23354, 29150

State Bank of India
M G Marg
Ph 26091

Medical Services

Ambulance

STNM Hospital
Ph 102 / 22944

Reiyukai Ambulance Service
Tibet Road
Ph 24228

Lions Club Ambulance Service
Ph 28487 (day) 26024, 21288 night

Hospitals

Central Referral Hospital
Tadong
Ph 31137, 32041

STNM Hospital
Ph 102, 22944

24-hour Chemists

Chiranjilal Lalchand
M G Marg
Ph 23762

Radiant
STNM Hospital

Communications

Post Offices

Head Post Office
P S Road,
Ph 22449, 23085, 25442

Deorali Post Office
Ph 23256

Raj Bhawan Post Office
Ph 23257

Courier Service

DHL
Green Hotel
M G Marg
Ph 20431, 29150

DTDC
MG Marg
Ph 28652, 28653

ELBEE
Green Hotel
M G Marg
Ph 20431, 29150

Gati Ltd
Deorali
Ph 81401

Overnite Express
New Market
Ph 23813

Speed Post EMS
(Govt-run)
All Post Offices

Cyber Café

There are many cyber cafés all over Gangtok, from where one can easily access the Net.

Long-distance Calls

Like all Indian cities, Gangtok, too, has innumerable telephone booths offering both domestic long-distance call facilities (called STD) or international (ISD) long distance calls.

WHAT TO BUY

Temi Tea
Sikkim Liqueur
Gingerina (Ginger paste)
Alpine Cheese
Dansberg Beer
SITCO watches
Handmade paper
Handicrafts
Black Cardamom (*Bara elaichi*)
Thankas
Carpets
Choksee
Passion Fruit Juice
Orchids (Hybrid)
Jams and preserves
Chilli pickle
Fresh bamboo shoots
Glass beads
Semi-precious stones
Handwoven jackets
Silver jewellery

Nurseries

Beyul Nursery
Rumtek
Ph 23486, 26089, 52213

Hidden Forest
Sichey Busty
Ph 23196, 25197

Himalayan Flora & Biotech
Development Area
Ph 22223, 25438

Wayside Gardens & Nurseries
6th Mile
Ph 50706, 50704

Curios

Charitrust Tibetan Emporium
P S Road
Ph 23468 ext 123

Curio Craft Gallery
P S Road
Ph 25739, 25368

Gift Shop
M G Marg
Ph 25113

Kandoika
New Market
Ph 28115

K C Somani & Sons
M G Marg
Ph 23635, 23534

Mandala Gift Centre
M G Marg
Ph 27319

Sikkim Art Emporium
NH 31A
Ph 27106

Sikkim Sarda & Co
M G Marg
Ph 23594

Snow White
M G Marg

State Handicrafts Showroom
Zero Point

Where to Stay

Gangtok has numerous hotels offering service ranging from indifferent to efficient. Don't expect appurtenances available in the metros but the hotels still make for a comfortable stay. Bookings for several hotels can be done in Delhi. Contact Sikkim Tourism, New Sikkim House, 14 Panchsheel Marg, Chanakyapuri, New Delhi Ph 6881976

Rs 2,000 & above

Netuk House
Tibet Road
Ph 22374, 26778

Norkhill Hotel
P S Road
Ph 25637, 25639

Tashi Delek
New Market
Ph 22038, 22991

Rs 1,000 - 2000

Bayul
M G Marg
Ph 24649

Central Hotel
Opp. Super Market
Ph 22105, 22553

Cherry Guest House
Church Road
Ph 25431, 29652

Chumbi Residency
Tibet Road
Ph 26618-19

Golden Nest
Namnang
Ph 27008, 27035

Heruka
NH 31A
Ph 80073, 80793

Rendezvous
NH 31A
Ph 26271-74

Swagat
P S Road
Ph 24295, 27751

The Oriental
New Market
21180-82

Tibet
P S Road
Ph 22523, 24962

Rs. 500-1,000

Anola
M G Marg
Ph 24233, 23238

Denzong Inn
Lall Bazaar
Ph 22692

Dew Pond
P S Road
Ph 23905, 27292

Glacier Guest House
M G Marg
Ph 22137, 28561

Gochala
Kazi Road
Ph 23634

Golden Nest
Namnang
Ph 27008, 27035

Golden Pagada
M G Marg
Ph 26928-29

Hungry Jack
NH 31A
Ph 28138

Magnolia
NH 31A
Ph 24687, 27749

Marigold
NH 31A
Ph 23951, 24089

Migtin
M G Marg
Ph 24101

Mintokling Guest House
Bhanu Path
Ph 24226

Mist Tree Mountain
P S Road
Ph 23827, 24263

Mount Jopuno
P S Road
Ph 23502, 28239

Mount Simvo
Tadong
Ph 31976

Mylong
Pani House
Ph 80446

Norbu Ghang
P S Road
Ph 22237, 23537

Park Residency
Near Super Market
Ph 28410-11

Pineridge
Namnang
Ph 24958

Pomra
Secretariat Road
Ph 26648

Sonam Delek
Tibet Road
Ph 22566, 28906

Soyang
New Market
Ph 22331

Staywell
NH 31A
Ph 23563

Sukhim Guest House
Namnang
Ph 23796, 27272

Sunny Guest House
NH 31A
Ph 22179

Teesta Rangit
New Market
Ph 25609, 28335

The Dzong
M G Marg
Ph 20278-79, 20281

The Four Seasons
Namnang Road
Deorali
Ph 81105, 80288

Tip Top (Gujarati Food)
D P H Road
Ph 26229

View Point
NH 31A
Ph 22549, 28579

Woodland
NH 31A
Ph 23414

Zam-Den
Old Children Park
Ph 24997

Zi
Tibet Road
Ph 25481

Below Rs 500

Alaya
Zero Point
Ph 25316

Annapurna
New Market
Ph 24877

Bayul
M G Marg
Ph 24649

Ben
New Market

Gangtok Lodge
M G Marg
Ph 26562

Green
M G Marg
Ph 24439, 25057

Holiday Hill
P S Road
Ph 22750

Kabur Inn Lodge
Tibet Road
Ph 27149

Kanchen View
Pani House
Ph 81762, 80763

Kanishka
Opp. Bus Stand
Ph 24011, 24690

Lhakar
P S Road
Ph 25708, 27082

Nahan Lodge
Church Road
Ph 28241

Natraj
Deorali
Ph 80799, 80550

New Green
Balwakhani
Ph 24060

Pomra Lodge
Bhanu Path
Ph 23479, 26648

Primula Lodge
Church Road
Ph 25496

Siddhrath
New Market
Ph 21009, 24807

Twilight Lodge
NH 31A
Ph 24352, 23225

Yumthang
Church Road
Ph 23841

Paying Guest

A couple of families take in tourists as house guests:

Borong House
Above Telephone Exchange
Ph 23473, 26822

Kewzing Home
Lower Development Area
Ph 23702, 25735

Resorts

There are a couple of luxury resorts in and around Gangtok. These all have aesthetically designed traditional cottages, with attached bathrooms fitted with all modern amenities. Given the increase in tourist traffic, more resorts are being established in the countryside around Gangtok. For a true pastoral taste of Sikkim coupled with tranquility these resorts are worth a try.

Martam Village Resort
Upper Martam
Ph 36843, 23314

Shambhala Mountain Resort
Rumtek
Ph 52240, 52243

The Blue Sheep

Sikkimese food is delicious but is essentially a variation on a single theme – *momos*. You can have these little flour dumplings steamed or fried; filled with pork, chicken, vegetables or even yak cheese. Any which way, they are finger-lickin' good. Also, try and get a taste of the local delicacy *Chetse-Detse*, a kind of pasta fried in yak butter, with mushrooms and shredded chicken thrown in.

Where to eat

Blue Poppy
New Market
Ph 22038, 22991

Café Tibet
NH 31 A
Ph 26363

Café Tibet
Kazi Road
Ph 21269

China Palate
New Market
Ph 27815

Crispy Cuisine
New Market
Ph 22766

Crystal Room
P S Road
Ph 23827

Dawat
M G Marg
Ph 20733

Dragon
M G Marg
Ph 25057, 24439

Dragon's Den
M G Marg
Ph 24649

Eden Park
NH 31A
Ph 28410-11

Ganesh Bhojnalaya
M G Marg

Glenery's
Metro Point

Gufa
L M Road
Ph 22692

Sher-e-Punjab
Arithang Road
Ph 22823

House of Bamboo
M G Road
Ph 29390

Jordy's Restaurant
Tibet Road
Ph 23469

Khana Khazana
M G Marg
Ph 20221

Krishna Restaurant
NH 31 A
Ph 28550

Marwari Bhojanalya
M G Marg

Moti Mahal
New Market
Ph 24430, 23998

Metro Fast Food
NH 31A
Ph 23245

Oberoi's Barbeque
New Market
Ph 23215, 27884

Orchid Café
NH 31A
Ph 29665

Parivar
M G Marg
Ph 27409, 24088

Porky's
Deorali
Ph 80702

Porky's
Development Area
Ph 26205

Porky's
New Market
Ph 31209

Quickbite
New Market
Ph 24709

Risur
Deorali
Ph 81007

Rush Hour
M G Marg
Ph 20278-79

Snow Lion
P S Road
Ph 22523, 23468

RUMTEK

Rumtek is situated 24 kms away from Gangtok in the Ranipul Valley. The *gompa* is open for visitors between 8 am and 5 pm.

How to get there

Rumtek is an hour's bus ride from Gangtok. Cars and Jeeps can be hired from Lall Market, and are also available on a sharing basis. Walking is a good option if you want to take in the spectacular views.

Where to stay

Martam Village Resort
Upper Martam
Ph 36843
Email martam@dte.vsnl.net.in

Sangay Hotel
Near Rumtek gompa

Shambala Mountain Resort
Ph 52240, 52243
Fax 52241, 23570
Email sikkim@ahmedindia.com

Tandoor
NH 31A
Ph 22179

Tea House
Tibet Road
Ph 26618-19

The Blue Sheep
M G Marg
Ph 29028

Tibet Kitchen
M G Marg

Unique
NH 31A
Ph 23881, 24134

Wild Orchid
NH 31A
Ph 22553, 22105

Lists of travel agents, hotels, restaurants and shops supplied by Sikkim Tourism.

PHRASE-BOOK

English – Nepali

In Emergencies

I feel unwell	*ma shacho chaina*
Please call a doctor	*daktar boliadhinohos*
Where is a hospital?	*aspital kati taadhaa chha*
Help	*guhaa*
I have fever	*malai jwaro ai kochha*

Useful Words

greetings	*namaste*
yes	*haan*
no	*nahin*
thank you	*dhanyabad*
day	*deen*
night	*raati*
morning	*bihaana*
evening	*saaj ha*
afternoon	*diuso*
tomorrow	*bholi*
hour	*ghanta*
food	*khana*
tea	*chai/chiya*
water	*pani*
hot water	*tato pani*
girl	*keti*
husband	*longne*
I	*ma*
you	*timi*
we	*haami*
my	*mero*
want	*chahanu*
please	*kripya*
see	*dekhnu*
why	*kina*
where	*kaha*
when	*khaile*
how much	*kati*
buy	*kinnu*
market	*haat*
closed	*bandh*
bad	*kharap*
good	*asal, raamro*
cold	*chiso*
diarrrhoea	*disia, lagun*
fever	*jwaro*
medicine	*dawai*
help	*madhat garnu*
hurt	*chot laagnu*
pain	*dukheyo*
lost	*haraayeko*
luggage	*jhola*
porter	*bhariya*
arrive	*aaipugnu*
house	*ghar*
toilet	*charpi*
move	*hino*
stop	*roko*
straight ahead	*sidaa*
left	*baya*
right	*daya*
north	*uttar*
south	*dakshin*
west	*paschim*

Essential Phrases

What is this?	*Yo ke ho?*
Where can I stay here?	*Mo kaha basno sak cho?*
Where will I get food?	*Ramro khana kaha payoncho?*
How are you?	*Sanchai chha?*
I am well.	*Thik chha.*
See you again.	*Pheri betaunla.*
How much is it?	*Kati rupiya?*
Do you have a room?	*Baas paainchha?*
How far is…	*Kati taadhaa chha…*
Where is…	*Kahaa chha…*

English – Hindi

In Emergencies

help!	*bachao!*
stop	*rukho*
medicines	*davai*
Please call a doctor/ambulance	*Doctor/ ambulance ko bulaiye*
Where is the nearest hospital?	*Nazdeek hospital kahan hain?*
I'm not feeling well	*Meri tabiyat theek nahin hai*
Where is... ?	*Kahan hai...?*
When will...be back?	*...vaapas kab ayenge?*
Call the police	*Police ko bulaiye*

Useful Words

hot	*garam*
cold	*thanda*
good	*achha*
bad	*bura*
open	*khula*
close	*bandh*
left	*baayen*
right	*daayen*
near	*paas*
far	*dur*
up	*oopar*
down	*neeche*
outside	*bahar*
inside	*andar*
fast	*jaldi*
slow	*dheere*
car	*gaadi*
bus	*bus*
road	*sarak*
way	*raasta*
house	*ghar, makaan*
door	*darwaaza*
fan	*pankha*
electricity	*bijlee*
train	*train, rail gaadi*
aeroplane	*hawai jahaj*
greetings	*namaste/namaskar*
yes	*haan*
no	*nahin*
thank you	*dhanyavad/ shukriya*
money	*paisa/rupaye*
time	*samay*
day	*din*
night	*raat*
morning	*subah*
evening	*shaam*
afternoon	*dopeher*
today	*aaj*
tomorrow	*kal*
yesterday	*kal*
here	*idhar/yahan*
there	*udhar/wahan*
food	*khana*
water	*paani*
girl	*ladki*
boy	*ladka*
woman	*aurat*
man	*aadmi*
who	*kaun*
why	*kyon*
what	*kya*
where	*kahan*
when	*kab*
how	*kaise*
one/two	*ek/do*

Essential Phrases

How are you?	*Aap kaise hain?*
Very well, thank you	*Hum theek hain, dhanyavad.*
What is your name?	*Aap ka naam kya hai?*
My name is...	*Mera naam...hai.*
See you.	*Phir milenge*
What is the time?	*Kitna baja hai?*
Where are you from?	*Aap kahan se aaye hain?*
Do you speak English?	*Kya aap angreji bolte hain?*
I don't understand	*Main nahin samjha.*
Please speak slow.	*Aap dheere-dheere boliye.*

INDEX

N
C H I N A
T I B E T
N E P A L
Zemu Glacier
Green Lake
Jakthang
Siniolchu
Khang-chen-dzonga
Kabru
Dzongri
S I K K
Tsokha
Bakhim
Yuksam
Khechopalri Lake
Tashiding
Pelling
Pemayangtse
Ravangla
Gyaltshing
R Teesta
Dentam
Hilley
Namchi Bazaar
Rang
Sombaria
Naya Bazaar
R Rangeet
R Teesta